T0284115

Russian Politics: A Very Short Introduction

VERY SHORT INTRODUCTIONS are for anyone wanting a stimulating and accessible way into a new subject. They are written by experts, and have been translated into more than 45 different languages.

The series began in 1995, and now covers a wide variety of topics in every discipline. The VSI library currently contains over 750 volumes—a Very Short Introduction to everything from Psychology and Philosophy of Science to American History and Relativity—and continues to grow in every subject area.

Very Short Introductions available now:

For more information visit our website:

www.oup.com/vsi/

Brian D. Taylor

RUSSIAN POLITICS

A Very Short Introduction

OXFORD
UNIVERSITY PRESS

Oxford University Press is a department of the University of Oxford.
It furthers the University's objective of excellence in research, scholarship,
and education by publishing worldwide. Oxford is a registered trade mark of
Oxford University Press in the UK and in certain other countries.

Published in the United States of America by Oxford University Press
198 Madison Avenue, New York, NY 10016, United States of America.

Library of Congress Cataloging-in-Publication Data
Names: Taylor, Brian D., author.
Title: Russian politics : a very short introduction / Brian D. Taylor.
Description: New York, NY : Oxford University Press, 2024. | Series: Very
short introductions | Includes bibliographical references and index.
Identifiers: LCCN 2024022806 (print) | LCCN 2024022807 (ebook) | ISBN
9780197516027 (paperback) | ISBN 9780197516058 (epub)
Subjects: LCSH: Political culture—Russia (Federation) | Russia
(Federation)—Politics and government—1991-
Classification: LCC JN6695 .T39 2024 (print) | LCC JN6695 (ebook) | DDC
306.20947—dc23/eng/20240611
LC record available at https://lccn.loc.gov/2024022806
LC ebook record available at https://lccn.loc.gov/2024022807

Integrated Books International, United States of America

For Anatol and Lucian

Contents

List of illustrations

Acknowledgments

Golfo Alexopoulos, Renée de Nevers, Maria Lipman, Robert Otto, James Richter, Valerie Sperling, and two anonymous reviewers gave me very valuable feedback on draft chapters. The Maxwell School at Syracuse University granted me a research leave that was essential to starting this project. I thank Simon Saradzhyan and the Russia Matters team at the Kennedy School of Government, Harvard University, and Xiaoxia Huang for help with the data and visualization for Illustration 6. Yulia Bychkovska provided research and editorial assistance, and Caroline Wazer prepared the index. I thank Nancy Toff, Rada Radojicic, and the rest of the Oxford University Press team for the faith placed in me by asking me to write this book and working with me through the process. It can take a long time to write a "very short" book.

Preface

Russian politics, like politics everywhere, is about how a human community allocates things of value among its members. This community has to set rules and establish a system of authority to make decisions. Political institutions—such as constitutions or electoral procedures in a democracy—set the rules of the game for members of a society as they engage in conflict, cooperation, and deliberation about values and resources. More simply, the American political scientist Harold Lasswell said that politics is about "who gets what, when, how."

In many countries, however, including Russia, the formal rules of the game are often not the main forces shaping politics. Instead, Russian politics since the mid-1980s has been dominated by outsize personalities such as Mikhail Gorbachev, Boris Yeltsin, and Vladimir Putin, who often could change or ignore the formal rules as necessary. Powerful leaders represent a source of potential dynamism and change in a political system in which formal institutions are weak and rules are meant to be bent or broken. At the same time, Russian politics is also powerfully shaped by larger, impersonal forces such as geography, Russia's place in the international political and economic system, and social composition and change. These larger forces tend to produce more predictable rhythms and persistent challenges.

A constant lodestar in Russian politics is the primacy of the state—the set of political and administrative organizations that make and enforce the rules and provide order in a given territory. To some, including Russia's current rulers, this primacy is a fundamental feature of political reality that is essential to the country's success. To others, it is an unfortunate historical pattern that must be overcome through society asserting itself in relation to the state for Russia to succeed in the future.

The collective "West"—Western and Central Europe and North America—also looms large in Russian history and politics. The West can be a source of inspiration, of threat, or of competition, but for centuries it has been a constant presence that shapes Russian political behavior and ideas.

Today, Russia is still working its way through the consequences of the revolutionary moment of the late 1980s and early 1990s, when one country (the Soviet Union) died and Russia and 14 other new countries were born. When something revolutionary happens, it overturns old ways of doing and seeing things and remakes whatever the object is—music, a branch of knowledge, a country. Think about what changed in a few short years. The borders of the Russian state are very different from those of both the Soviet Union in the twentieth century and the Russian Empire in the eighteenth and nineteenth centuries. Consequently, the number of citizens is much smaller as a percentage of the world's population than in the past and more ethnically homogeneous than before. These people are forging a new national identity that draws on some, but not all, elements of the country's past. A multinational empire fell apart, and its core successor polity is still struggling to become a coherent and stable multinational state.

Russia's place in the world is different because of this revolution and the simultaneous imperial collapse—it has reverted to being merely a "great power" after decades as a "superpower." Moreover, that superpower (the Union of Soviet Socialist Republics) represented a radical alternative in economic and political life, a system variously called "socialism" or "communism." The centrally planned economic system of state socialism was abandoned in favor of building a capitalist system based on a mix of private and state property and integration into world markets. A political system built around Communist Party domination of all spheres of life has given way to a different form of authoritarianism that mimics the forms of electoral democracies and, until recently, had more modest ambitions of social control than the USSR had.

This revolutionary transformation powerfully shapes Russian politics. Although Russia's history can be traced back centuries, the relative newness of its current political system makes it quite different from countries whose borders and constitutional order have endured relatively unchanged for much longer. Russia has had only two rulers since the new country was created. Boris Yeltsin accomplished some very fundamental things in helping to destroy the old order and create a new one, but ultimately his political fortunes were swamped by the force of the cataclysm. His successor, Vladimir Putin, played a key role in helping the new order stabilize early in his rule, while also changing its features and policies in major ways. Many Russians now see no real alternative to Putin as ruler and give him credit for Russia "rising from its knees" during his rule. His domestic critics contend that he has built a corrupt authoritarian system that is stagnating at home and exceedingly reckless abroad.

The Russo-Ukrainian War, which started in 2014 but took on a significantly more full-blown and violent nature in 2022, may prove to be nearly as politically consequential for Russia as the 1991 Soviet collapse. The Russian state became much more repressive, and the economy was remilitarized. Once again, the very borders of the country are in doubt, with Putin illegally claiming Ukrainian territory and others arguing that Russia might disintegrate if it loses the war.

At some point Putin will leave the Kremlin, but his departure will be driven either by political upheaval or basic biology, not by a free vote of the Russian people. The new ruler will inherit a barrelful of challenges. The central question will be a recurring one: Should they try to rule over the people as subjects, or govern with the consent of, and in the interests of, the people as citizens?

Chapter 1
Governing the world's largest country

Two simple geographic facts are a great starting point for understanding Russia. First, Russia is very big. Second, Russia is very cold. Russia sits astride the Eurasian landmass, accounting for more than one-tenth of the world's land surface. The Russian national anthem proudly proclaims:

> From the southern seas to the polar lands
> Spread our forests and fields.
> You are unique in the world, one of a kind.

Geography has powerfully shaped Russia's political system over time. Russia's immense scale and difficult climate led its rulers to seek to centralize control to keep the country from falling apart. The creation of a transcontinental and multinational empire reinforced these centralizing impulses. The downfall of that empire in 1991 with the demise of the Soviet Union opened up the possibility for Russia to become a more decentralized and democratic federal political system. Russian President Vladimir Putin has behaved as if the country is in danger of further collapse, leading him to undermine a federal system that might be the best way to govern a country of Russia's scale, complexity, and multiethnic population. Today, climate change is presenting new challenges to Russia's political and economic development.

Moscow is the capital and the largest city in Russia; today, its greater metropolitan area is home to about 20 million people, or almost one-seventh of the entire population of the country. It is the center of road, rail, and air travel networks. Geographically, it is not the physical center of the country, which is much farther east. But it is fitting that Moscow is Russia's political and economic center, because it was from the medieval principality of Muscovy that the country that would become Russia began to grow roughly 700 years ago.

In the thirteenth and fourteenth centuries, much of the territory that is now part of Russia, including Moscow, was controlled by the Mongol Empire, ruled by the descendants of Genghis Khan. The principality of Muscovy started to accumulate power as a tax collector for the Mongol Empire. The Russian Orthodox Church moved its seat from the nearby town of Vladimir to Moscow in 1325. As the power of the Mongol Golden Horde waned in the fifteenth century, Muscovy's territorial reach grew. Its location on the Moscow River in the basin of the Volga, Europe's longest river, provided a good vantage point to expand its control over adjacent lands as the Mongols retreated back into Asia. One example of the growing power of Muscovy that still stands today was the construction of the red brick walls of the Moscow Kremlin during the reign of Grand Prince Ivan III ("the Great") in the late fifteenth century.

Ivan III's grandson, Ivan IV, was crowned "Tsar of All the Russias" at the age of sixteen in 1547. This event symbolically marked the transition from the medieval principality of Muscovy to the early-modern state of Russia. It was under Ivan IV, commonly known as Ivan the Terrible but perhaps more accurately translated as Ivan the Formidable, that Russia conquered the Tatar city of Kazan, roughly 400 miles to the east, and began its expansion into Siberia. Saint Basil's cathedral, built in Red Square next to the Kremlin, commemorated the defeat of the Kazan Tatars. By 1650, Russia had spread its territory all the way to the Pacific Ocean, making it the world's largest contiguous land empire.

Muscovy's rise was in many ways surprising. Because of the cold climate, relatively poor soil, and short growing season, the area around Moscow was sparsely populated. It was far from the major hubs of world commerce, especially because it lacked access to major maritime trade routes, but also because the traditional overland trade routes between Europe and Asia were much further south. Culturally, it also was relatively isolated from important civilizations such as China, the Islamic Middle East, and Western European Catholicism.

At the time of Ivan the Terrible, Russia was in no position to successfully challenge European countries to the west, but Siberia to the east was a different matter. "In Europe we were hangers-on and slaves," the Russian writer Fyodor Dostoevsky would proclaim several centuries later, "whereas in Asia we shall go as masters." The imperialist sentiment is clear. Fewer than 200,000 native peoples, primarily consisting of hunters, gatherers, and nomads, lived in Siberia (northern Asia between the Ural Mountains and the Pacific Ocean) around 1600, an area of over 5 million square miles. No great powers were competing with Russia for this territory.

The process of Russian geographic expansion continued for several more centuries, although not at the same precipitous pace by which Russia conquered Siberia. The going was tougher as Russia looked to the west, southwest, and south, directions in which the climate was better and the competition was fiercer. Russia established control over Kyiv (Kiev in Russian) and eastern Ukraine in the late seventeenth century. Tsar Peter I ("the Great") opened a "window to Europe" in the early 1700s by defeating Sweden in the Great Northern War and acquiring territory around the eastern and southern shores of the Gulf of Finland. Peter moved the Russian capital to his new namesake city of Saint Petersburg, located at this outlet to the Baltic Sea. At the end of the 1700s, Catherine II ("the Great") extended Russian control south to the northern shores of the Black Sea after a successful war with the Ottoman Empire, and then agreed on the partition of

3

Poland with Prussia and Austria, extending Russia's border as far west as Warsaw. In the nineteenth century, Russia expanded to the Caucasus and Central Asia in the south and also acquired further territory from China in the Far East. By 1900, Russia covered one-sixth of the earth's land surface.

Ruling a Eurasian empire

This litany of territorial expansion is simultaneously impressive and misleading. There was nothing inevitable about Russia's geographic growth, and it is a mistake to think that Russia was somehow uniquely expansionist. The period of Russia's expansion, roughly between 1550 and 1900, took place more or less at the same time as the rise of Western Europe to global dominance and the spread of European imperialism around the globe. Acquiring new territories and exploiting them for resources, and competing with other countries for foreign lands while trampling on the rights of the indigenous populations, was typical behavior for Europe's major powers.

Russian imperial expansion differed in important ways from that of its European peers. The "next door" nature of Russia's geographic spread made it less dramatic, perhaps, and often less noticeable. Russians moved into new territories over land or along rivers, not across oceans. There was no clear and obvious separation, administratively speaking, between Russia proper and its newly acquired territories. The fact that the empire was next door and part of the same ecosystem also meant that the native local populations were less susceptible to being decimated by unfamiliar diseases, as happened in the Americas, although smallpox also took a deadly toll among the indigenous populations of Siberia in the seventeenth century. Russia extended its rule over peoples that had different ethnic backgrounds, spoke different languages, and worshipped differently: Tatars, Buryats, Estonians, Ukrainians, Uzbeks, Georgians, Yakuts, Chechens, and many others. This is the essence of colonial empires.

4

Russian imperialism was driven by a mixture of economic, geopolitical, and cultural motives. Siberia was especially important economically. Furs were a key source of revenue for the tsarist government, and conquered indigenous groups had to pay fur tribute to the tsar. Later, iron ore from the Urals helped build Peter I's military, and other natural resources such as timber, gold, coal, diamonds, oil, and gas were key sources of revenue for Imperial Russia and the Soviet Union; they remain important for post-Soviet Russia. Ukraine was important for both agriculture and mining.

Geopolitics and the quest for security were especially critical motives in Russian expansion. The traditional heartland of Russia around Moscow is on the plains of Eastern Europe and not protected by any natural barriers, such as mountains or seas. In both the early 1600s and early 1800s, external invaders (first Poland, then Napoleonic France) occupied Moscow before eventually being driven out. During World War II, Nazi Germany surrounded and blockaded Leningrad (Saint Petersburg) for 900 days and advanced to within 20 miles of the Kremlin in Moscow. To the south and southwest, competition with the powerful but declining Ottoman Empire persisted for several centuries. Eastern Europe was a tough neighborhood.

Because it is the world's largest country, and situated in a relatively harsh climate, Russia's population density is quite low compared with Europe to the west, Turkey and Iran to the southwest, and China to the southeast. The combination of immense size and relatively low population meant that Russia often struggled to defend its borders, which were long, far away, and relatively easy for invaders to penetrate, given the absence of natural barriers. Moreover, many of the people living in frontier areas were not ethnically Russian or Orthodox Christian. Russia's rulers had good reasons to be concerned about the loyalty of these subjects. Russian cultural and racist views about their superiority over non-Russians and especially non-Slavs also drove Russian imperial policies.

Russia's location, climate, and size made it difficult not only to protect itself, but also to enrich itself. Russia controls a lot of valuable natural resources, but its geographic conditions made the accumulation of wealth much more difficult than in Western Europe. European cities such as Venice, Amsterdam, and London, easily connected to global trade routes by sea, had a growing urban and commercial class. Rulers could bargain with bankers and merchants to acquire money to expand their armies while offering protection in return. In contrast, in remote Muscovy and then Russia, towns and cities were smaller. Further, Russia's climate and soil made agriculture more difficult than in much of Europe, meaning most people often lived on the edge of survival. That, too, made money and resources harder to come by, as there was little agricultural surplus to sell. Russia's tsars secured the resources needed to protect the state—and their own power—through the use of force and domination rather than through trade and bargaining. The tsars treated all of Russia's land as their own, distributing it as favors to members of the nobility who loyally served the state, including as officers of the imperial army. This service class of aristocratic warriors together with the ruling monarchy were the twin pillars of the Russian state.

Russia's vast size and harsh climate also complicated government control. It was difficult to build the transportation infrastructure, such as roads and railroads, to knit the country together and promote commerce and communication. "Russia suffers from its distances," Tsar Nicholas I is said to have complained. As Europe developed and its states became more powerful, they not only were better able to wage war with their neighbors and conquer faraway peoples, they also were able to monitor, tax, and communicate with their own citizens more efficiently. To compensate for its vast size, forbidding climate, and lower level of development, the Russian state tried to manage its population by controlling land and restricting mobility.

Russia's size and location have led to long-running—cynics might say tedious—debates about whether Russia is European, Asian, or something else. To which the correct answer is yes, yes, and once again yes. Russia is European because its historic core around Moscow is geographically in Europe, most of its population (75 percent) lives in the European part of the country, its primary language is a European language from the Slavic family, and the dominant religion is Christianity (Orthodoxy, the dominant religion in multiple European countries). Russia is also Asian. Seventy-five percent of Russia's territory is in Asia (beyond the Urals). Siberia— the Asian part of Russia—is fundamental to Russian identity. Many of Russia's natural resources that fuel its economy are in Asia. But Russia is also something else all its own. Geologically, Russia sits astride the Eurasian tectonic plate; there are not separate "European" and "Asian" plates. In that sense, separating Asia and Europe as distinct continents is a matter of convention more than anything. Although Russia is part of both Europe and Asia, it is on the northern periphery of both. This peripheral location meant that historically Russia was often a bystander to cultural, economic, and political developments in both of these continents.

Russia is thus simultaneously European, Asian, and something distinct. Russians themselves have often been conflicted about where they belong. Although as a matter of geography the issue is perhaps uninteresting, as a matter of cultural identity this debate is hundreds of years old and is not going away anytime soon. It is also bound up with politics. In the nineteenth century, for example, heated philosophical debates raged between "Westernizers" and "Slavophiles." Westernizers promoted the ideals of enlightenment, rationalism, individualism, freedom, and progress. Slavophiles— literally "lovers of Slavs"—rejected Westernization, which they saw as a disease infecting Holy Russia. Slavophiles were conservative nationalists who emphasized Russia's Orthodox and collectivist traditions and its separate and distinct path.

The Asian direction for Russia is not just a matter for cultural debate but also a matter of economics and foreign policy. Under the last two tsars, the construction of the Trans-Siberian Railway was intended to link Russia's Asian population more tightly to the rest of the country, and also to serve as an important east-west trade route. Although Russia's population has always been concentrated in its European heartland, over time the population did spread eastward. Most of this settlement of the Asian part of Russia took place during the Soviet period (1917–1991). The Soviet government deliberately sought to shift more people into Siberia. It did so for multiple reasons, including the desire to exploit its natural resources, geopolitical concerns about protecting its far-flung territory, and a commitment to industrialize the entire country. The Soviet state used its coercive power and centralized planning apparatus to enact this policy, including sending millions of citizens to work in the inhuman Soviet forced labor camp system known as the Gulag.

This Soviet policy of encouraging population settlement in the Urals and Siberia was a mistake. The geographic distribution of Russia's population is a fundamentally unnatural legacy of misguided Soviet policies and represents a "Siberian curse" for its current government. The Soviet Union exacerbated the problems that Russia faces by virtue of being big and cold by moving people and industry to even colder places that are especially costly to access. This increased transportation costs, labor costs (people are less productive when cold), equipment costs (equipment breaks down more easily), housing and utility costs, and so on. Russia has always faced high production costs due to its size, remoteness, and climate; the Soviet government made the problem worse.

Other northern countries, such as Canada and the Scandinavian countries, have not made these mistakes. In these countries, most people live in the south of the country or along the coast. Ninety percent of Canadians live within 100 miles of the border with the United States. Canada, the country perhaps most similar to Russia geographically—continental in scope, very far north, and rich in natural resources—uses seasonal labor in its northern territories, rather than trying to build large cities there. Thus, the nine coldest cities in the world with a population over 1 million are all in

Russia. This misallocation of resources and people is just one of the costly legacies of the Soviet period.

The too-brief federalism experiment

If the Soviet legacy of permanently putting millions of people where they should not live is an obvious burden, a second important Soviet geographic legacy has more complicated effects. That legacy is the decision to organize Russia politically as a federation. A federation is a political system in which decision-making power is divided between central and regional governments (states in the United States, for example). Countries with multiple ethnic groups or nationalities sometimes opt for what political scientists call ethnofederalism, which provides some level of political autonomy to these different ethnic groups; examples of this include Canada, India, and Nigeria. Constitutionally, Russia today is an ethnofederal state, with some regions at least formally designated as the homeland of non-Russian ethnic groups.

Imperial expansion over the centuries extended Russian rule over many other ethnic groups and nationalities and religious communities. This was not a political problem for quite a while. But in nineteenth-century Europe the ideology of nationalism was spreading. Nationalism is based on three core ideas. First, it holds that humanity is made up of different nations, which are communities of people who share kinship based on factors such as shared language, culture, ethnicity, or history. Second, nations are the main repository of political legitimacy. Third, each nation should have political autonomy, most commonly an independent state, and members of the nation owe loyalty to this state and community. The unification of Germany and the unification of Italy, both in 1871, redrew the map of Europe and showed the political potency of nationalism.

If nationalism was a solution for Germans and Italians, it was a political problem for the rulers of multinational empires such as Russia. By 1897, ethnic Russians made up only 44 percent of the

9

population of the country. The strength of nationalist sentiment varied widely across the different nationalities in Imperial Russia, but nationalism as one potential organizing principle of political life was in the mix in the political upheaval brought about by World War I, the Russian Revolution of 1917, and the subsequent civil war. Notably, the other land empires of Europe—Imperial Germany, the Austro-Hungarian Empire, and the Ottoman Empire—collapsed at this time. Most of the Russian Empire, in contrast, continued under a new name, the Union of Soviet Socialist Republics (USSR).

The faction that ultimately won the revolution and civil war, the Bolsheviks, was a socialist political party whose members believed that class identity was more important than ethnic or national identity. At the same time, their leader, Vladimir Lenin, had described Imperial Russia as a "prison house of nations" and advocated self-determination for non-Russian nationalities. The Bolsheviks adopted the principle of ethnofederalism for the new socialist state, which it called "a free union of free nations, as a federation of Soviet national republics." Member republics formally had the right to secede.

For most of the period of Soviet rule, the federal nature of the country was largely a fiction. The strong centralized control of the Communist Party of the Soviet Union (CPSU) meant that the republics that made up the Soviet Union did not have meaningful decision-making power. Even so, the federal structure of the Soviet Union was not irrelevant. Especially in the 1920s and early 1930s, but also somewhat thereafter, the CPSU promoted the development of local languages and cultures and the promotion of officials from the "titular nationality" (i.e., Ukrainians in Ukraine, Armenians in Armenia, Uzbeks in Uzbekistan, and so on). At the same time, the Soviet state cracked down harshly on expressions of nationalist sentiment not endorsed by the CPSU. Under Joseph Stalin, particularly in the 1930s and 1940s, various ethnic groups and nationalities were subject to forced deportations, starvation, purges, and executions.

In the end, the decision to organize the Soviet Union as a federation with national republics contributed greatly to making nations that would later form the basis of independent states when the Soviet Union collapsed in 1991. The simplest and most obvious way for the USSR to end was for each of the 15 republics—Russia, Ukraine, Kazakhstan, etc.—to become independent states. "The Soviet Union resembled a chocolate bar," observed one former Soviet official. "It was creased with the furrowed lines of future division, as if for the convenience of its consumers."

The largest republic in the Soviet Union was Russia. The Russian Soviet Federative Socialist Republic (RSFSR) represented about 75 percent of the geographic area of the Soviet Union, 60 percent of the economy, and roughly half of the population (147 million out of 286 million). But, to turn the equation around, in one day, on December 31, 1991, the Russian empire "lost" 25 percent of its historic territory, half of its population, and 40 percent of its economy. The Soviet Union was not Russia, but much of the lost territory had been part of Russia for over a century. This territory was greater than the entire size of the European Union, and Russia's borders reverted to about what they had been 300 years earlier, at the time of Peter I.

One curious feature of the Soviet federal system was that it was also what Russians refer to as *matryoshka* federalism, after the nesting dolls in which a wooden doll has a series of smaller dolls inside. Thus, several of the Soviet republics, including the RSFSR, had a federal system inside of them. Newly independent Russia, then, was born federal, and this status was reflected in the new December 1993 constitution. Russia's federal system is particularly complex. It has more than 80 subunits—more than any other federation in the world.

Unlike in the United States, where all the subunits are called states and have identical legal status with respect to the federal government, in Russia there are no fewer than six types of subunits, with some variation in their legal status. The most basic

11

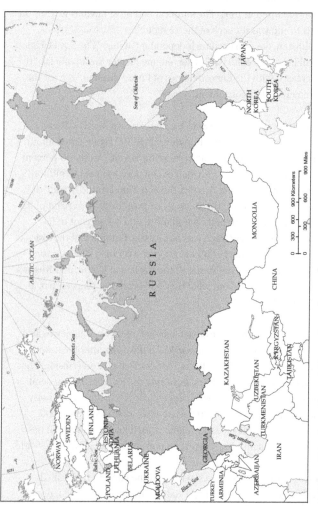

1. Map of Russia and its neighbors after 1991, with the 15 republics of the Union of Soviet Socialist Republics all becoming independent states. Russia has used force to alter the borders of Georgia and Ukraine, but these changes are not internationally recognized.

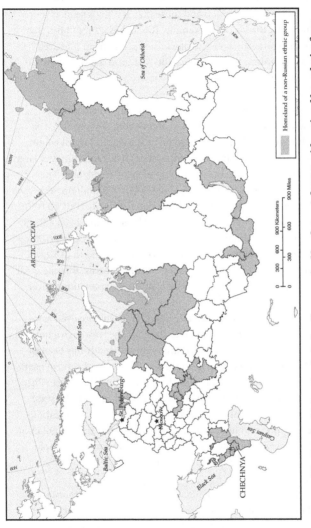

2. Map of the Russian Federation in its legally recognized borders as of 2024, with regional boundaries from that year. The shaded regions are those named after non-Russian ethnic or national groups, reflecting Russia's multinational and multiethnic society.

Homeland of a non-Russian ethnic group

distinction, reflecting the principle of ethnofederalism, is between those regions that are considered the homeland of a particular non-Russian ethnic group and those that are lands seen as more traditionally Russian. For example, Russia has 22 republics that are named after the non-Russian ethnic group from that area (Tatarstan, Komi, Buryatia, etc.) and that have the right to their own constitution and language.

There is a great deal of variation across Russia's regions in key attributes such as population, size, and wealth. For example, the Republic of Yakutia in Siberia would be the eighth-largest country in the world if it was an independent state; it is 2,000 times as large as the smallest region, the federal city of Saint Petersburg. The federal city of Moscow has a population of over 10 million, whereas the Nenets Autonomous Okrug has a population of about 40,000. And because of its small population and large oil and gas holdings, the economic wealth of the Nenets Autonomous Okrug in 2018 was more than $100,000 per person, compared with less than $2,000 for the Republic of Ingushetia in the North Caucasus. Russia's great size encompasses a great deal of diversity at the subnational level.

This incredible size and diversity has often been perceived as a major headache for whoever rules the country. How do we hold this together? The instinct of Russia's rulers usually has been to seek to control everything from the top. The tools of control have often been coercive, enforced by the military and the police. Firm, centralized control has partially been an illusion, with the state not having the resources in terms of personnel, communications infrastructure, and bureaucratic capacity to really dictate policy at the local level. The state was powerful and primary, but people often found ways to outwit or evade control.

Geography may be a reason for adopting centralized authoritarian rule in Russia, but it also serves as an excuse. Other countries that are hard to govern due to their size and diversity have often opted for sharing power through federalism rather than trying to centralize it in the capital. Examples of this approach include the United States, India, Canada, Australia, Nigeria, Malaysia, and Brazil. Some politicians in post-communist Russia embraced the notion that shared power and strong regions might make the system of government more effective than the traditional over-centralization approach preferred by the tsars and the communists. Russia may have been dealt a bad hand in terms of being so cold and so remote, but Russia was not doomed to autocracy; climate and geography influence political outcomes, but they do not determine them.

During the 1990s, Russian federalism was both an experiment and a work in progress. Russia had no previous experience with democratic federalism. In stable democratic federal systems, institutions such as the written constitution, the courts, and political parties help maintain a healthy balance between the central government and the regions. Russia had a brand new and contested constitution, a weak rule of law, and feeble political parties. President Boris Yeltsin (1991–2000) had originally told the regions to "take as much sovereignty as you can swallow," but that was more of a slogan than an actual policy. He had to negotiate a series of deals with regional governors to try to balance demands for greater autonomy with the need to preserve the supremacy of the central government on essential issues.

The threat of further state breakdown, with regions leaving independent Russia the same way the other 14 republics had left the Soviet Union, was on many people's minds. Even before the Soviet Union was finished, the republic of Chechnya in the North Caucasus had declared itself independent. In December 1994 President Yeltsin took the fateful step of launching a military attack against Chechnya, unleashing a two-part anti-secessionist war (1994–1996, 1999–2009) that eventually would result in the death of as many as 100,000 people.

The Chechen wars had multiple causes. Arguably one of the most important ones was the determination of both Boris Yeltsin and his successor, Vladimir Putin, to not allow one of Russia's regions to gain independence, fearing it would unleash a further unraveling of Russia. Putin envisioned a process starting in the North Caucasus that would run "up the Volga [river]. . . . Straight into the heart of the country." He said that when he came to power it was his "historic mission" to deal with the violence in the North Caucasus and "stop the collapse of the country."

Was the territorial integrity of Russia at risk in the 1990s? Could it have unraveled as the Soviet Union did? Might it do so in the future? There were certainly some causes for concern. First, the post-Soviet Russian state was very weak. Communist Party control held the Soviet Union together, and that system was now gone. Second, the economy plummeted into a serious depression lasting most of the decade. This depression not only deprived the government of money but also convinced some regions that they might be better off on their own, particularly regions that were rich in natural resources. Third, parts of Russia are quite culturally and ethnically distinct from the Russian majority population.

Overall, however, the risk of further territorial disintegration was and remains low. Three factors are key: ethnic composition, economic self-sufficiency, and geographic location, specifically an external border. The population today is 80 percent ethnically Russian; in contrast, only half of the population of the Soviet Union had been Russian. Although it still has quite a diverse population and territory conquered centuries ago from non-Russian ethnic groups, Russia is much more homogeneous now than it has been for several centuries. Even in most of the officially designated ethnic republics, the "titular" ethnic group does not represent a majority.

Economics and geography also make the disintegration of Russia unlikely. The vast majority of Russia's regions—more than 80 percent—are dependent to some degree on transfers from the federal budget. Moreover, some of the ethnic republics are landlocked. If we count up the regions where there is a majority non-Russian population, an external border, and a population of greater than 1 million people, there are only two that meet all of those criteria—Chechnya and its neighbor Dagestan. These two republics are two of the poorest and are heavily dependent on Moscow for subsidies. Thus, despite the fear of Russia's rulers that Chechnya could be a domino that would start the disintegration of the country, it was really a special case rather than the harbinger of a larger pattern.

Vladimir Putin's determination to "stop the collapse of the country" led him to pursue centralizing policies that he called the "strengthening of vertical power." He introduced a series of changes in the nature of Russian federalism, all designed to give more power to the central government and weaken the autonomy of the regions. He appointed "presidential representatives" for different areas of the county whose job was to make sure that federal agencies at the local level worked for the central government rather than for the regional governors. Another important change took place in the economic sphere, where the share of taxes that went to the regions declined from 50 percent to 30 percent during Putin's first two terms as president (2000–2008).

The most consequential change in the Russian federal bargain took place in 2004 and was related to the wars in Chechnya. On September 1, 2004, a group of terrorists from the North Caucasus seized a school in the town of Beslan, taking over 1,000 hostages. The hostage crisis ended in a chaotic and bloody battle that left more than 300 people dead, more than half of them children. In the aftermath of the tragedy, Putin announced his intention to cancel elections for regional governors and appoint them directly instead. There was no obvious connection between the Beslan terrorist attack and governor elections, but it offered an opportunity for Putin to further strengthen the control of the central government over the regions. Governor elections were resumed in 2012, but with a "filter" in place that makes it very hard for opposition candidates to get on the ballot, let alone win.

Overall, Russia's experiment with a genuine and balanced form of federalism to try to govern a large and diverse country was short-lived. If the pendulum swung too far toward decentralization in the 1990s, since then it has swung too far in the opposite direction. Although on paper Russia remains a federation, in general the emphasis under Putin has been on securing Moscow's control and minimizing regional autonomy. He has reverted to the approach of the tsars and the Soviet communist leaders, who relied on centralization to hold Russia together.

Federalism as a political system often has a bit of a chicken-and-egg feel to it: Are federations hard to govern because of their federal structure, or are they federal because the nature of the underlying society makes them hard to govern? The noted political scientist Alfred Stepan once claimed that for a large, multinational state to be a democracy it must be federal. That seems too categorical, but it is true that most large, multinational democracies in the twenty-first century are federal. Going forward, genuine federalism might yet prove to be a viable form of governance for Russia if it becomes more democratic.

The effects of a changing climate

Russia was, is, and will remain very big, but it is becoming less cold due to climate change. Indeed, because of Russia's far northern location, it is warming at more than twice the global average. Since 2000, Arctic temperatures have risen at more than three times the global pace, primarily because less snow and sea ice mean less sunlight is reflected back into space.

At first glance, it might seem that Russia would be better off as the planet heats up. Russia's cold climate has presented difficult challenges for its development and governance throughout its history. And the Russian government has suggested several possible benefits to Russia of a warming climate, including more land available for agriculture production, easier access to natural resources in the far north, and especially increased shipping in the Arctic Ocean.

The strong scientific consensus, however, is that climate change will be as bad for Russia as for the rest of the planet. Even some of the potential benefits, like expanded agriculture production, are likely to be offset by more frequent droughts in other areas. Negative consequences that Russia is likely to face include increases in extreme weather events such as forest fires, super storms, droughts, heatwaves, and floods. Russia could also confront new parasites and diseases as the planet warms.

The biggest internal climate change problem for Russia, which also has global implications, is the melting of permafrost. Around 60 to 65 percent of Russian territory is in permafrost areas. As Russia's climate warms, this permafrost is melting. Melting permafrost threatens existing infrastructure, including housing, commercial buildings, roads, heating systems, and energy-sector infrastructure, including pipelines. Even more significantly, the melting of Russia's permafrost will release more greenhouse gases into the atmosphere, including methane and carbon, creating a feedback loop in which rising temperatures cause permafrost melt and the further warming of the atmosphere.

Despite the threats to Russia from climate change, the Russian government's response has been desultory. President Putin has bad-mouthed strategies to mitigate climate change, stating that "I think humanity could once again end up in caves, simply because it won't consume anything." Russians have always taken pride in their ability to cope with, and even thrive in, the country's forbidding climate. This tendency went into overdrive in the Soviet period, during which a belief in the ability to use science and technology to harness nature for the good of socialist development led to considerable environmental damage. In contemporary Russia, the economic importance and political influence of the oil and gas sector, as well as a political system that shuts out the small and weak environmental movement, has made it a bystander to the global effort to fight climate change. In the coming decades, as the global economy transitions away from coal, oil, and gas, Russia's resource-dependent economic model will struggle mightily to adapt. The 2022 Russian invasion of Ukraine accelerated Europe's effort to wean itself off of Russian hydrocarbons. This global energy transition toward renewable energy will threaten Russia's great power status, a key point of pride for the country for three centuries.

Chapter 2
Power, status, and greatness

International politics are generally neither equal nor fair. It is common to presume, both in scholarly books and casual speech, that some combination of power and status gives some countries a special place in global politics. For hundreds of years, these countries have been referred to as "great powers." This designation is usually understood to reflect some combination of population, size, resources, economic prowess, and military might. Although the lines sometimes can be blurry, there are only three countries in the world that international relations experts typically classify as having been a great power for the past 300 years: Britain, France, and Russia. Some great powers have been in the club for less time, such as China and the United States. Other countries that were once considered great powers—Spain, Austro-Hungary, the Ottoman Empire—no longer exist or no longer warrant the designation. Russia, without a doubt, is a country that matters in international politics.

When the Soviet Union broke down in 1991, and especially after a decade of economic decline in the 1990s, some observers asked whether Russia would remain a member of the great power club. One American journalist declared in 2001 that "Russia is finished," undergoing an "unstoppable descent of a once great power into social catastrophe and strategic irrelevance." This possibility haunted Russia's new president at the time, Vladimir

Putin. In his annual state of the nation speech in 2003, he linked the fate of the country to its great power status: "All of our historical experience shows that a country like Russia can live and develop in its existing borders only if it is a great power. In all periods when the country was weak—politically or economically—Russia always and inevitably faced the threat of collapse." It matters to Russia that they matter.

Many average Russians agree that maintaining great power status is important for the country. Voters in multiple surveys have indicated that making Russia a "respected great power" should be a top goal of the country's president. Furthermore, Russians believe Putin has delivered on this ambition, rating this as one of his greatest achievements. When he came to power in 2000, nearly two-thirds of Russians did not consider the country a great power; 20 years later, more than two-thirds believed that it was.

As the largest country in the world, and one of the two leading nuclear powers (Russia and the United States possess nearly 90 percent of the world's nuclear weapons), Russia certainly remains one of the great powers. At the same time, by economic and demographic criteria, Russia today is weaker than it has been in 300 years. By these measures Russia also lags far behind the two leading powers, China and the United States. The effort to maintain great power status continues to be an important driver of Russian foreign policy. It was also one source of Putin's 2022 invasion of Ukraine, a disastrous war that will weaken Russia's global position for the foreseeable future.

Great power to superpower

Russia became a great power under Peter I ("the Great"). Russia's defeat of Sweden in the Great Northern War in 1721 was the breakthrough to Europe that Peter had been working toward his entire reign. Achieving the status of a European great power was not easy, nor was maintaining it. Economically and socially, Russia lagged behind Western Europe in terms of income, literacy, technological development, and public health. Geographic factors weighed heavily on Russia's ambitions. Although Peter I secured an outlet to the Baltic Sea, and Catherine II ("the Great") later in the eighteenth century established one on the Black Sea, Russia's geographic core still remained far from the main European trade routes of the Mediterranean and the North Atlantic. Still, these conquests helped connect Russia to the rest of Europe and reduced Russia's relative isolation.

Russia's large and expanding territory and population gave it some obvious military advantages. Its size made it difficult for any invader to conquer. Its population meant that it could put more men under arms than its rivals. On the other hand, there also were drawbacks to expansion. Increasing Russia's territory did not stabilize its borders and make them easier to defend, but more the opposite—it pushed them even further from the Russian heartland, making protecting and communicating with distant frontiers more difficult. Furthermore, conquering neighboring territories brought peoples of different ethnicities, languages, and religions into the empire. This became an increasing problem in the nineteenth century as ideas of national self-determination and democratic rule spread.

Another serious challenge to Russian power in the nineteenth century was the Industrial Revolution, which fundamentally changed the nature of war. After winning most of the wars it had fought for a century and a half from the early eighteenth century forward, Russia's defeat in the Crimean War (1853–1856) showed how far it lagged behind leading European powers technologically. The Russians shot muskets with a range of 200 yards at foes who had rifles that could fire five times as far.

Things went from bad to worse for Russia at the beginning of the twentieth century in terms of great power politics. Russia was the most populous of the European great powers and had by far the biggest military, with more than one million men under arms. But Russia was still overwhelmingly a peasant society with low levels of literacy, and economically it lagged behind its competitors. The strain of World War I (1914–1918), in which Russia, Britain, and France fought against Germany, Austria-Hungary, and the Ottoman Empire, led to the end of tsarism, sparking the Russian Revolution of 1917. The communist revolutionaries who ultimately seized power in October 1917 initially expressed disdain for traditional great power competition and withdrew Russia from World War I. The revolutionary leaders Vladimir Lenin and Leon Trotsky believed that international working-class solidarity was more important than patriotism, and they hoped that seizing power in Russia could be the trigger for socialist revolutions in the more developed countries of Western Europe. New socialist governments would then cooperate to end war, capitalism, and imperialism.

History did not turn out that way. Socialist revolutions did not spread across Europe. Civil war engulfed Russia until 1921. The victorious communists proclaimed the formation of a new country, the Union of Soviet Socialist Republics (USSR). They had lost control over Poland, Finland, and the Baltic states of Estonia, Latvia, and Lithuania, but retained much of the rest of the Russian Empire. Fears about the potential threat to the young socialist state from the capitalist great powers waxed and waned in the 1920s and 1930s, but the prospect of war was never absent and was one of the chief reasons for Joseph Stalin's late 1920s forced industrialization drive. "To slacken the tempo would mean falling behind," Stalin stated in 1931, "[a]nd those who fall behind get beaten."

World War II—called the Great Patriotic War in the Soviet Union, and in Russia today—was an existential threat to the young communist country, and indeed the biggest military challenge that Russia had ever faced. The USSR initially entered the war in 1939 on the side of Nazi Germany, conquering the Baltic states and seizing parts of Poland and Romania as part of a pact between Stalin and German dictator Adolf Hitler. Two years later Hitler double-crossed Stalin, invading the Soviet Union in June 1941. Germany pushed deep into Soviet territory, overrunning all of Belarus and Ukraine, blockading Leningrad (Saint Petersburg), and advancing to within 20 miles of the Kremlin in Moscow. The Soviet Union eventually prevailed, with some important help from its allies, Great Britain and the United States, but at a dreadful cost. Roughly 25 to 27 million Soviet citizens died during the war. The Germans murdered 2.5 million Jews on occupied Soviet territory—40 percent of the 6 million Jews exterminated during the Holocaust. Thousands of towns and tens of thousands of villages were completely destroyed during the war. The Great Patriotic War was simultaneously a great national triumph and a great national tragedy.

In terms of great power politics, the results of World War II elevated the Soviet Union to a unique position. It was now a "superpower," with equal status to the United States. No longer was it the lone communist country in a world of capitalist states; it was now the leader of the communist bloc. The Soviet Union imposed compliant governments in occupied Eastern European countries such as Poland, Hungary, and Czechoslovakia. Communist governments also came to power in Asia, most importantly in China in 1949. Communism, which stretched from Berlin to Beijing, was on the march globally, seemingly vindicating communist ideology's claim that it would overtake and replace capitalism.

In important respects, the Cold War was not an equal fight, and the Soviet Union was plagued by many of the conditions that had bedeviled the Russian tsars. Most obviously, the USSR lagged well behind the United States and its allies in overall economic and technological development. In 1950 the US economy was roughly three times as large as that of the Soviet Union, and even stronger in per capita terms. Moreover, most of the other wealthiest countries were allied with the United States, such as Britain, France, West Germany, and Japan. As in the past, the Soviet Union compensated for this economic gap by pouring resources into the military (and related fields such as space). It was able to match the United States in these areas, but at the cost of slowly falling further behind in terms of broad-based economic development.

The Soviet Union also faced the challenge, like tsarist Russia before it, of trying to hold together a large, multinational empire. Russians made up only about half of the total population of the Soviet Union. This problem was compounded after World War II, when the Soviet Union constructed an "outer empire" of communist Central and Eastern European allied countries to go with its "inner empire." This outer empire, acquired as a buffer zone to protect the Soviet heartland, proved to be a source of frequent instability during the Cold War, with anti-communist movements in countries such as Hungary and Czechoslovakia triggering Soviet military intervention. Eventually, Soviet leader Mikhail Gorbachev (1985–1991) determined that the political and economic costs of controlling the outer empire were too much, and 1989 witnessed a cascade of successful anti-communist revolutions throughout the region. In 1991 the multinational empire known as the USSR also collapsed, several months after the failure of a hardliner coup designed to overthrow Gorbachev and stop the nationalist independence movements in many of the republics.

A diminished great power

Imperial Russia and the Soviet Union had an impressive run. A country on the northern periphery of Eurasia had risen slowly and seemingly inexorably from a marginal country in global politics to one of the core European great powers, and then to one of the two global superpowers. During the Cold War, the Soviet Union had the world's second-largest economy (after the United States) and third-largest population (after China and India). In 1992 independent Russia reverted to roughly the size it had been under Peter I. It inherited the Soviet Union's nuclear weapons and UN Security Council seat, but it was now much smaller in terms of territory, population, and economy.

The massive decline in Russian power meant different things to different people. Many in the West heralded a "new world order" in which peace and democracy would reign and great power competition would become a thing of the past. In Russia, however, the loss of power and status was a source of resentment and humiliation. In hindsight, Western euphoria and optimism at the Cold War's end was excessive. The 1990s were what the journalist Charles Krauthammer called a "unipolar moment," when the United States was clearly the dominant world power. Since that time, China has surged and Russia has recovered sufficiently to invest heavily in rebuilding its military. By 2017 the US National Security Strategy identified a return to "great power competition," naming China and Russia as "revisionist powers" seeking to change the existing international order. Russia's 2022 invasion of Ukraine showed its revisionist aims in stark terms.

Not everyone agrees that Russia is a great power comparable to the United States and China. Historically, two of the major drivers of great power status were the size of a country's population and the size of its economy. By these standards, Russia is weaker than it has been in more than 300 years. Russia now has about 2 percent of the world's population—and of its economy. Demographically, Russia peaked as a great power on the eve of World War I, when the Russian Empire represented nearly 9 percent of the world's population. Economically, Russia peaked as a great power in the 1950s and 1960s, when the Soviet Union represented roughly 10 percent of the global economy. Contemporary Russia is much weaker than its historic predecessors.

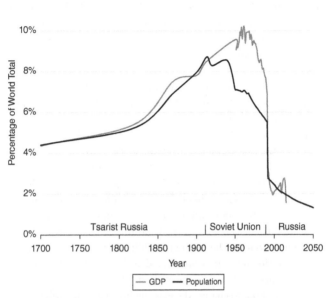

12%

10%

8%

6%

4%

2%

0%

Percentage of World Total

Tsarist Russia | Soviet Union | Russia

1700   1750   1800   1850   1900   1950   2000   2050

Year

— GDP — Population

3. Graph of Russia as a percentage of global population and global economy (gross domestic product) over the past 300 years. The graph shows data for the Russian Empire until 1917, for the Soviet Union between 1917 and 1991, and for the Russian Federation from 1992 forward.

By these two measures, Russia is also much weaker than both the United States and China. There are two basic methods to compare countries' economic size. If one is interested in how far a dollar or euro or ruble goes at home, then Russia has the sixth-largest economy in the world, but one that is more than five times smaller than that of China or the United States. If one is interested in what a ruble could buy in the international marketplace, then Russia's economy is ten times smaller than that of the US or China. It would not even make the top ten of world economies, lagging behind countries such as Italy, Brazil, and Canada.

Russia also trails quite a few countries in terms of its population. Russia's population is half that of the United States and a little more than one-tenth of China's. Russia now ranks ninth in the world, although it is still the most populous country in Europe. Its population ranking is projected to drop to fourteenth in the world by 2050 according to the United Nations, overtaken by countries such as Egypt, Mexico, and Tanzania.

Technological prowess might be another route to great power status in the twenty-first century. This is a category in which the United States excels, in which China traditionally lagged but recently has made great strides, and in which Russia does very well in some sectors but not consistently across all areas. Despite a well-earned reputation for scientific achievement, Russia is not competitive with the most economically developed countries in terms of broad-based innovation. There are no Russian equivalents to Apple, BMW, Samsung, or Huawei. The most successful "Russian" tech innovator is Sergey Brin, the founder of Google, whose family immigrated to the United States in 1979. The "brain drain" problem means that some of Russia's most talented and entrepreneurial people have left the country.

Perhaps Russia's most important advantage as a great power is geography, although this could be as much a liability as an asset. Nevertheless, its status as the world's largest country, geographically adjacent in the West to the European Union (EU) and in the East to China, Japan, and even the United States, gives it important influence in world affairs. Despite massive losses in the war against Ukraine, Russia retains considerable military power. Its large reserves of oil and gas—roughly 15 percent of total world reserves in both categories—have led some to dub it an "energy superpower." It has also been aggressive in developing its cyber capabilities and its global media presence under Putin.

In some ways the Russia of today is like its earlier incarnations—geographically massive, heavily militarized, and with a sizable population, but also possessing an economy that lags behind that of the leading great powers in the world. It plays an important role in global affairs and so should not be underestimated or dismissed. But, overall, it is a diminished great power compared with what it was in the nineteenth and twentieth centuries. It remains the dominant power in much of its neighborhood, although countries like China, the United States, and even Turkey are more active in the region than previously. Consider the status of Poland since 1900. Russia began World War I with much of Poland part of its territory and ended World War II with political and military control over Poland. Now, however, Poland is part of the North Atlantic Treaty Organization (NATO) and the EU and allied with Russia's two main twentieth-century rivals, Germany and the United States. The poor performance of the Russian armed forces in Ukraine has been a stark indicator of Russia's diminished power even in the military realm.

Finally, it is worth asking to what extent it matters today to be the world's largest country with a sizeable military. To be sure, many Russians take pride in the country's "greatness." But in other things that matter to citizens—a reasonable standard of living, health and longevity, access to knowledge—Russia performs respectably but is far from a world leader. According to the 2021 United Nations Human Development Index, Russia has "very high human development" and ranked 52nd in the world, roughly equal to countries such as Turkey, Romania, and Uruguay, and ahead of China (79), Brazil (87), and India (132). Yet it was far behind its traditional great power rivals such as Germany (9), the United Kingdom (18), Japan (19), the United States (21), and France (28).

The fight to survive

The Cold War ended with a Western victory more sweeping than imagined by the most resolute American hawks. Not only did the Soviet Union give up its external empire in Eastern Europe, but it also dissolved itself, renouncing its communist ideology. The country was financially broke and undergoing a deep political and economic crisis. Russia's new leader, President Boris Yeltsin, thought that the country needed friends more than enemies. His first foreign minister, Andrey Kozyrev, made clear who should be Russia's best friends: "The United States and other Western democracies are as natural friends and eventual allies of the democratic Russia as they are foes of a totalitarian U.S.S.R."

Kozyrev emphasized common democratic values and friendship. Yeltsin wanted to be part of the Western club, not on the outside looking in. This desire was both political and economic. His press secretary later remarked that Yeltsin believed that "[g]old rain would pour down on us, the borders would open, foreign goods would pour in all because Yeltsin was on friendly terms with the other leaders."

Things would not be so easy. The economic crisis would last the entire decade and was too large to be overcome simply with Western aid. Russian and American interests would clash during the Balkan Wars of the 1990s and over NATO's decision to accept some of the Soviet Union's former allies as new members. Furthermore, Russia intervened politically and sometimes militarily in ethnic conflicts in the former Soviet republics of Moldova, Georgia, and Tajikistan, and between Armenia and Azerbaijan. In 1996 Yeltsin replaced the face of Russia's friendly policy toward the West, Foreign Minister Kozyrev, with Yevgeniy Primakov, an influential foreign policy voice from Soviet times. Primakov pursued a policy guided less by friendship with the West and more by a desire to elevate Russia as an independent great power in a new multipolar world.

Vladimir Putin became president in 2000 and at first continued this policy. Russia's official foreign policy concept published in 2000 emphasized the country's status as a great power and its role in helping maintain a stable international order, the importance of neighborly relations along its perimeter, and the need for favorable external conditions to enable Russia to pursue internal reform and development. Russia's internal war with the breakaway republic of Chechnya and the related issue of domestic terrorism dominated the security agenda in Putin's first term. After the 9/11 terrorist attack on the United States, Putin quickly reached out to President George W. Bush to offer support. He suggested that the United States and Russia stand together in the fight against global terrorism, although the two countries sometimes disagreed on who's a terrorist.

By the end of Putin's first two terms as president, however, Russia's relations with the United States were strained. To Putin and Russia's leadership, the problem was that the United States was not prepared to treat Russia as an equal and create new global rules of the game that took its interests into account. Putin had a long list of complaints that he was happy to share with visiting Western officials and leaders, including about the 1999 Kosovo War, US missile defense programs, the US-led invasion of Iraq in 2003, and the ongoing NATO enlargement. The list grew longer in subsequent years.

To some observers, the downturn in Russia's relations with the West was an inevitable consequence of growing Russian power. The period of relatively good relations between Russia and the West lasted from the late-Gorbachev years through the early years of the Putin presidency, when Russia was uncharacteristically weak. Putin believed that Russia had become too dependent on the West, and he therefore used a windfall of petrodollars in the 2000s to pay off Russian debts to Western governments and banks. He thought once Russia was able to restore its economic sovereignty and then military power, it could more forcefully defend its interests as an independent great power. Defense spending had declined by more than 60 percent under Yeltsin, but during Putin's first eight years as president defense spending more than doubled. In time, especially after a major defense reform launched in 2009 and a large rearmament program in the 2010s, a rebuilt Russian military would give Putin a broader range of foreign policy options than those available to Yeltsin.

Greater economic and military power made possible some policy options that might have seemed unattainable previously. But foreign policy still involves choices, and there were important changes under Putin that cannot be linked solely to Russia's growing power. Most generally, in the early 1990s Yeltsin believed that, with the end of communism, Russia was on a path to becoming a democratic country that would be a natural ally of the leading democratic powers. He did not believe Russia was a "besieged fortress" under threat from hostile enemies, although he grew disappointed with the United States over time.

In contrast, President Putin and some of his closest associates in the Russian government on multiple occasions suggested that the United States was behind domestic upheaval in Russia and neighboring countries. For example, after the 2004 Beslan school attack, Putin obliquely blamed the United States for sponsoring the terrorists. He asserted, "We appeared weak. And the weak are beaten. They want to cut from us a tasty piece of pie, others are helping them. . . . Terrorism is only an instrument for achieving these goals." The statement was a distinct echo of Stalin's 1931 warning about the weak getting beaten. The issue of alleged American interference in Russia and its neighbors is an obsession of Putin and some of his closest advisers; rather than analyzing the domestic sources of disorder and discontent, they prefer to blame the meddling of outsiders.

Putin famously stated in 2005 that the end of the Soviet Union was "one of the greatest geopolitical catastrophes" of the twentieth century. It was specifically a "geopolitical" disaster because of what it meant for Russia's loss of power and status, which he was determined to recover. It was Putin's vision of Russia's proper place in the world that led to the buildup of Russia's military power, not the buildup of military might that caused a changing vision and policy.

Over time, Putin's Russia began to present a more menacing face to the world. In December 2014 Putin proclaimed that it was impossible for the Russian bear to "just sit quietly . . . and feed upon berries and honey." Its enemies, Putin said, wanted to "put [the Russian bear] in chains . . . and rip out his teeth and claws." Russia, he said, had to defend "our independence, our sovereignty, and our right to exist. . . . We want to survive and to fight . . . or we want our skin to hang on a wall. That is the choice we face." He offered no evidence that any great power sought to do this.

This harsh vision of a world in which Russia had to fight to survive was a traditional one. Some Russians tend to see their history as one in which over the centuries the country only survived by heroically fighting off powerful foreign aggressors, particularly from the West. This account has some truth to it. At the same time, it rests on the false notion that Russia only defended itself, rather than also engaging in conquest and colonization. The Soviet Union fell apart not because of external threats but primarily because of internal weaknesses, especially the difficulty of holding together a massive multinational empire. After the collapse of the Soviet bloc and the Soviet Union, Russia had indeed lost the buffer zone on its western periphery that it had acquired under the tsars and Soviet rulers. But it was not clear it needed one. After all, Russia possesses thousands of nuclear weapons, an overwhelming deterrent threat that makes direct invasion unthinkable. Moreover, international relations experts observed that in the post–World War II era, states rarely "die," especially through conquest. It was virtually impossible to imagine Polish or French or German armies marching upon Moscow as they had in centuries past.

Putin, however, saw a more threatening world, and one in which Russia was not being given its proper due. Over time, Putin's goal of reclaiming Russia's lost status and position in the world led to a series of fateful steps that changed Russia's relations with many countries and culminated with the 2022 full-scale invasion of Ukraine. Russian moves to change the borders of the neighboring countries of Georgia and Ukraine were consequential and a harbinger of the 2022 war. In 2008 Russian troops moved into the South Caucasus country of Georgia, after Georgia launched an attack on its breakaway region of South Ossetia. Russia quickly sent troops into two disputed Georgian regions, Abkhazia and South Ossetia. Russia, which had previously held the position that the borders of the former Soviet republics—including Russia—at the time of the Soviet dissolution were the internationally legal borders, changed tack and recognized Abkhazia and South Ossetia as independent countries. These two regions are now de facto Russian protectorates.

Putin's decision in 2014 to annex the peninsula of Crimea from Ukraine was even more important. This dramatic move followed a revolutionary change in government in Ukraine. In November 2013 then Ukrainian President Viktor Yanukovych, partially due to pressure and inducements provided by Putin, reneged on an earlier commitment to sign an association agreement between Ukraine and the European Union. Yanukovych's decision launched several months of street protests that culminated in a violent confrontation in the capital city of Kyiv in February 2014. When Yanukovych fled the capital on February 21, 2014, Putin decided that "we must start working on returning Crimea to Russia."

Russia's March 2014 illegal annexation of Crimea was the first military takeover of part of a neighboring state in Europe since the end of World War II. Putin, however, portrayed it as the righting of a historical wrong that left Crimea outside of Russia after the Soviet collapse. There was also a strong ad hoc and emotional component to Putin's decision: he was stunned by the breakdown of the Yanukovych government and, characteristically, blamed it on alleged US interference. After the Crimea annexation, Russia instigated and backed a proxy war inside southeastern Ukraine—an area known as the Donbas—in an effort to weaken Ukrainian statehood and provide Russia with another way of influencing Ukraine. Russia's overall goal was to keep Ukraine in its political orbit, but the annexation of Crimea and the Donbas war angered Ukrainians and pushed Ukraine toward the EU and the West. Over the next eight years, Putin failed repeatedly to force Ukraine to settle the Donbas war on his preferred terms, which would have given Russia a de facto veto over Ukraine's foreign policy orientation.

Putin's growing frustration with his inability to force Ukraine into the Russian sphere of control led to the most fateful foreign policy decision of his rule in February 2022—outright invasion of the entire country. From early in his presidency, Putin had expressed his concern about the possibility of Russia "losing Ukraine," and had noted his view that Ukrainians and Russians are "one people" and that Ukraine "isn't a real country." Twenty-two years into his rule, he opted for the most brutal approach to assert control over Ukraine, a war of territorial aggrandizement. In 2023 the International Criminal Court in the Hague charged Putin with the war crime of responsibility for the illegal deportation of Ukrainian children to Russia. Putin's quest to recapture lost status had culminated in a bloody and illegal war of imperial conquest.

Integration and isolation

Russia's full-scale invasion of Ukraine in 2022 led to the biggest rupture with the West since the Cold War. The United States and its European and Asian allies adopted harsh sanctions against Russia, the most far-reaching ever to be imposed on an economy as large as Russia's. In addition, thousands of companies either cut back their dealing with Russia or left Russia entirely. Europe sought to reduce its dependence on Russian energy—coal, oil,

Russian Politics

4. Citizens of Dnipro, Ukraine, look at a residential building destroyed by a Russian missile on January 22, 2023. The Russo-Ukraine war is the largest war in Europe since World War II.

and gas—going forward, an economic relationship that had been central to the Soviet and Russian economy for five decades.

The war against Ukraine threatens to reverse arguably one of the most important foreign policy achievements of Russia after the Soviet collapse—greater economic and cultural integration with the outside world. During the Cold War, Soviet citizens were largely cut off from the outside world. Most of them could not travel outside the communist bloc, and people behind what Winston Churchill in 1946 called the Iron Curtain had limited access to information and cultural products (books, movies, television shows, and so on) that were not formally approved by Soviet censors. Access to Western consumer goods was also tightly restricted.

All of that changed with the end of the Cold War. After a 75-year detour into the communist dead end, which in many ways constituted a different civilizational alternative, Russia returned to the world, and people, goods, and services moved relatively freely in and out of Russia. The rise of the Internet meant that Russians also had access to global information and culture at their fingertips. Russians texted on their iPhones and ate delivery sushi while watching Hollywood movies on their Korean televisions. Now, however, the prospect of a return to relative isolation was at hand, with Russia placing increasingly restrictive limits on the Internet and the free flow of information.

Of course, there will be no return to the Iron Curtain. For one thing, many members of the Russian elite established deep ties with the outside world. One of Putin's daughters lived in the Netherlands for years, his press secretary's daughter lived in Paris, and his foreign minister's daughter lived in the United States. Other economic, political, and cultural elites also became accustomed to a greater openness to the outside world. Russia is no longer the leader of an ideological project and a separate political and economic system, as it was during the Cold War.

There also will not be a new Cold War, at least not one like the last one. Russia is no longer an economic and military peer to the United States the way that the Soviet Union was (except in terms of nuclear weapons). Russia, unlike the Soviet Union, is not at the center of a major political and economic bloc, having few actual formal allies; for its war against Ukraine, it has been forced to buy ammunition and weapons from Iran and North Korea. Moreover, Russia is not trying to win a global bipolar competition. Instead, its goals are to establish a sphere of influence in Eurasia and to undermine what it sees as an unjust unipolar system centered upon the United States. To that end, Russia has promoted disinformation in Western countries in an effort to weaken them politically. Russia also used its cyber capabilities to hack and leak material meant to influence the 2016 US presidential election.

Russia is not alone in trying to change the existing international order. Most importantly, China has similar goals. The two countries have forged a close partnership based on this common aim of a multipolar world in which authoritarian governments are not the target of criticism due to their domestic political situation. They are united in opposing the current "liberal international order" in which the United States and its allies play a dominant role. Any fears that Russia might have about its more economically dynamic and populous Asian neighbor are seen as less important now than their shared goals and worldview.

Despite the breakdown in Russia's relations with the West, globally the picture is more mixed. In addition to the strong relationship with China, Russia participates in a variety of international fora in which it maintains cooperative relationships with countries such as India and Brazil. Russia is a major player in the Middle East, intervening in Syria in 2015 to save the Syrian government from potential overthrow and maintaining connections with such important and diverse countries as Turkey, Iran, Israel, Saudi Arabia, and Egypt. Only four countries supported Russia's 2022 invasion of Ukraine in the United Nations, and 140 countries opposed it. But 38 countries abstained, including the world's two most populous countries, China and India.

Russia, especially its political leadership, feels itself to be a victim of an unfair loss of power and status. Putin portrays a dangerous world in which Russia's sovereignty is under threat. Russia's geographic size, nuclear weapons, and permanent UN Security Council seat guarantee its continuing great power status. For much of Putin's rule, he could make a credible case that he was rebuilding Russian power and that Russia was "rising from its knees" and standing up to its enemies, especially the United States. Yet the greater economic power of the United States, the European Union, and China, as well as rising countries such as India, Indonesia, Brazil, and Mexico, meant that Russia's future standing in the world remained in doubt even before the

Russo-Ukraine War. Now, the damage to Russia's political reputation and long-term economic and military power caused by the invasion of Ukraine has undermined these earlier foreign policy achievements. Also in question is Russia's development trajectory, which for centuries has been based on the goal of catching up with the West.

Chapter 3
Playing economic catch-up

Russia's massive size and northern location make it geographically unique. Its 300-year history as a modern great power gives it a status in international politics held by only a handful of countries. Economically, on the other hand, Russia is less exceptional. Russia, like more than 50 other countries in the world, is considered an "upper-middle-income" country by the World Bank. Its peers include countries such as Brazil, China, Indonesia, Mexico, and Turkey.

Today, Russia is comparatively richer than the majority of countries in the world but poorer than the great powers it historically compared itself to, such as Britain, France, Germany, and the United States. This has long been true, and catching up economically has explicitly been a goal of multiple Russian and Soviet leaders. The Union of Soviet Socialist Republics (USSR) pioneered a novel path to economic development that some called socialism or communism but might best be described as a centrally planned or command economy. The Soviet Union said it would not only catch up with but ultimately overtake the world's leading capitalist countries. It never came close to achieving this goal outside of a few select areas, such as armaments and the space race, and eventually it threw in the towel.

This distinct developmental path still influences Russia's contemporary economic and political system, more than three decades after Russia reversed course and adopted a capitalist economic model. The socialist legacy is what makes Russia notably different from most countries that have roughly the same level of wealth. In the 1980s Russia did not have such fundamental capitalist features as private property, market prices set by the fluctuation of supply and demand, commercial banks, unemployment, bankruptcy, and so on. It acquired most of these things in a big rush in the early 1990s.

Russia's economy has a series of features that stifle development and tend to reinforce authoritarian politics. These include a high dependence on exports of natural resources, especially oil and gas; high wealth inequality; a weak rule of law and high levels of corruption; and a state that plays a large and frequently harmful role in the economy. These features stand in the way of realizing the long-standing goal, also embraced by President Vladimir Putin early in his reign, of catching up with wealthier countries. In fact, since 2014 the economy has stagnated and Russia is falling further behind.

The communist experiment

At the turn of the twentieth century, Russia was an overwhelmingly peasant country. On the eve of World War I in 1913, 70 to 80 percent of Russian laborers were in the agriculture sector. The comparable figures were 12 percent in Great Britain, 28 percent in the United States, and 40 percent in France. Compared with most European states, Russia came late to the Industrial Revolution. In the last decades of the Russian Empire, the state played an important role in stimulating industrialization and economic growth by erecting trade barriers to protect industry and investing heavily in building railroads. Large cartels dominated key sectors such as steel and coal, and the tsar's permission was needed for certain projects. Russia's rulers understood that its economy needed to change and industrialize in order to keep up with its rivals, but they feared the socioeconomic changes that came with development, and they therefore sought to control the process.

The turmoil of global war, revolution, civil war, and famine between 1914 and 1922 massively disrupted Russian economic growth and development. Roughly 10 percent of the population died during this period, and millions more emigrated. It took until 1927 for the economy to return to the level it had been at in 1913 on the eve of World War I. Fully 87 percent of the Soviet population worked in agriculture in 1927, a higher percentage than before the war. The self-proclaimed "workers' state" had few industrial workers.

Soviet dictator Joseph Stalin came up with a radical new economic approach that changed the Soviet Union, and indeed the world, forever. The two main pillars of the new command economy were forced industrialization in line with a central plan and the collectivization of agricultural lands and livestock under the control of the communist state. The Soviet leadership launched these two policies in 1928 and 1929 in what has been called Stalin's "revolution from above." Stalin argued in a 1931 speech that forced industrialization must be pursued as quickly as possible, because "those who fall behind get beaten." To avoid this fate, Stalin claimed that the USSR "must put an end to its backwardness in the shortest possible time. . . . We are fifty or a hundred years behind the advanced countries. We must make good this distance in ten years. Either we do it, or we shall be crushed."

Soviet rulers did not know exactly what a socialist economy should look like—Karl Marx provided no roadmap—but they knew it should not look like a capitalist one. Marx and his coauthor Friedrich Engels stated plainly in *The Communist Manifesto* that "the theory of the Communists may be summed up in the single sentence: Abolition of private property." And that is what Stalin's policies did, with some minor exceptions. Industrial enterprises and collective farms were given production targets from a Five-Year Plan, rather than responding to market incentives of profit and prices that fluctuated in response to supply and demand.

The human costs of this project of social and economic engineering were immense. Roughly seven million people died in the famine brought about by collectivization and forcible seizures of land, grain, and livestock. In a very crude way, however, the end result of this chaos and suffering was what Stalin wanted—millions of former peasants became workers, and the Soviet Union made what some economists call a "Big Push" toward industrialization. Between 1928 and 1940, about 20 percent of the labor force moved from agriculture to other sectors of the economy. Stalin expanded the forced labor camp system greatly at this time, as "anti-Soviet elements" were deported to the far corners of the empire to lay railroad tracks, mine gold and coal, and fell timber. The economy grew rapidly, especially in the priority area of heavy and military industry, with industrial production increasing at around 10 percent per year from 1928 to 1940. However, economists are sharply divided about whether Stalin's strategy can be considered a "success" even in strictly economic terms. Some argue that forced industrialization propelled the Soviet Union to begin catching up with the developed capitalist countries. Others counter that the entire process was highly inefficient and that a more gradual and less disruptive process could have achieved similar results.

The Soviet economic model was unlike anything the world had ever seen before. Capitalist countries regulated aspects of their markets, and sometimes directly intervened in production—this was particularly common when they were at war. But the Soviet Union went far beyond those forms of state intervention in the economy. It created a command economy in which land and property were owned by the state, production decisions for the entire economy were made by the state, and prices were set by the state. The novelty of the system was noted by the very first chairman of Gosplan, the state planning agency, who observed that the system was based on "the implicit assumption that the government possesses some magical power that enables it to cater to all needs in whatever proportions are considered desirable."

Millions of peasants moved to cities and became industrial workers. Massive factories sprang up around the country to produce iron and steel that workers would transform into trains, ships, tanks, planes, and tractors, and equally massive dams were built to generate electricity. Over time it became clear just how misguided and costly some of these decisions were, such as building factories that were too big to be efficient—sometimes labeled "gigantomania"—in the wrong places. Ideological concerns and not the needs of the population drove economic planning.

The Soviet Union undoubtedly did become more "modern" than tsarist Russia in the sense this word is often used by scholars— literate, educated, and urban. Literacy increased from 57 percent in 1926 to 99 percent by 1979, and urbanization increased from 17 percent in 1926 to 69 percent in 1979. Women entered the workforce in unprecedented numbers: the female workforce increased by 16 times between 1928 and 1970. Life expectancy at birth increased from around 45 in the mid-1920s to over 68 by the end of the 1950s, although going forward these numbers leveled out.

Russia's development trajectory must have been extremely disorienting for average people. On the eve of World War I, Russia was an overwhelmingly peasant country ruled by a monarch. A little more than three decades later, the country had changed its name, redrawn its borders multiple times, and endured a series of cataclysmic events: two massive world wars and one civil war, two horrific famines, a political revolution that installed the world's first avowedly socialist government, and a second revolution engineered from above that transformed the economy and was accompanied by immense violence and political terror. Tens of millions of people died from unnatural causes, namely starvation and violence. Almost everyone had their lives radically transformed. It was an enormous national trauma. Yet at the end of three decades of cataclysms, the country achieved a momentous wartime victory in the Great Patriotic War and rose to the status of global superpower at the vanguard of the world communist movement.

By the 1970s, however, the communist economic model had reached its limits. The fundamental problem was that the Soviet path to development and modernity was flawed—it is better characterized as mis-development or mis-modernization. It relied on the rapid and forced input of additional labor (by moving people from farms to factories) and physical capital (by building new factories, machines, and equipment). People making economic decisions—whether central planners, factory managers, or foremen on the shop floor—did not have to worry much about efficiency. Quantity mattered more than quality. Once the shift from a predominantly agricultural economy to an industrial one was over, the primary task should not have been to add more inputs but to use the existing ones more efficiently and to increase labor productivity. But Soviet-style socialism was bad at that; a firm would not go out of business because its products were inferior, and workers were for the most part not likely to get fired because their work was subpar. "You pretend to pay us," went the Soviet expression, "and we pretend to work." Creativity and innovation were discouraged, and entrepreneurship was criminalized; fulfilling the plan—even if this meant falsifying the data—was what mattered. Collectivization had severely damaged the agriculture sector, so grain and other products were imported. The fact that so many resources were devoted to the military—around 15 to 25 percent of the economy—made matters worse.

The Soviet economy never functioned properly. Shoppers often had to queue for basic foodstuffs like milk, meat, and butter. Millions of people—including a young Vladimir Putin growing up in Leningrad in the 1950s and 1960s—lived in so-called communal apartments where the entire family shared one bedroom and the toilet and kitchen were shared with multiple other families. Most people's standard of living was well below that of people living in the advanced capitalist countries; Soviet gross domestic product (GDP) per capita in the 1970s was between 35 and 40 percent of the US level. In the 1970s an aging Soviet leadership was able to put off economic reforms because world oil prices skyrocketed, bringing in considerable cash from the global sale of Siberian oil. Efforts by the last Soviet leader, Mikhail Gorbachev, to "restructure" the economy by introducing some market elements to the planned economy were too little, too late, and actually made things worse. The flaws of communism for average people, not only in the USSR but throughout the communist bloc, were captured in the succinct complaint of a Polish worker in the 1980s: "Forty years of socialism, and there's still no toilet paper!"

What did 60-plus years of the Soviet economic experiment ultimately deliver for the country as a whole? At first glance it might appear that socialism to some extent "worked"—the Soviet Union had the second-largest economy in the world from the 1930s to the late 1980s. Yet in a long-term perspective, compared with other countries in the world, Russia ended up roughly where it had been before the revolution. The former Russian politician and economist Yegor Gaidar observed that Russian economic performance fluctuated over the past 150 years, but in general Russia has lagged about 50 years behind the most developed countries in the world. In other words, Russian economic growth for a century and a half has been "at the average world level." Other economists have shown similar results. If the Russian economy is compared to other world economies from 1900 to 2000, it actually became less complex and its exports less diverse and sophisticated from the first period to the second. Finally, Russia and the other post-Soviet states paid a severe price when exiting communism and returning to capitalism in terms of a protracted economic depression, high inflation, and material deprivation for many citizens.

The return to capitalism

Having embarked on the historically unique task of building a communist command economy in the 1920s, Russia reversed course in 1992 and set about building a capitalist market economy. Russia was one of several dozen post-communist countries in Eastern Europe and Eurasia that began the road back from communism to capitalism. Reformers generally understood the process as a return to the global economy after decades of creating an economic system that sought to be largely separate and self-sufficient. They hoped that Western governments and experts would help, and outside advisers rushed in. The problem was that although there was plenty of world experience with modern capitalism, there was not much knowledge about how to turn a communist economy into a market one. The former Polish President Lech Walesa gave the following analogy: "It is easy to turn an aquarium into fish soup, but not so easy to turn fish soup back into an aquarium."

The fundamental tasks identified by economic reformers were referred to as privatization, liberalization, and stabilization. If communism meant the abolition of private property, then capitalism meant its restoration. If a command economy meant centralized planning, then capitalism meant, as the Scottish philosopher Adam Smith said, the "invisible hand" of the market. Liberalization, then, was letting people and firms exchange goods and services at prices set by supply and demand. This exchange of goods could also take place beyond a country's borders, which meant the liberalization of trade and making national currencies convertible into other currencies—the ability to trade dollars for rubles, or vice versa, for example. Finally, stabilization refers to the need to try to fight runaway inflation during the transition process by controlling the money supply and state spending.

This short list—privatization, liberalization, and stabilization—obscures the reality of hundreds of different changes needed to create a modern capitalist economy. Doing these three things successfully also required a long-term fourth process, building institutions, which meant creating new economic rules of the game, along with organizations to referee compliance with the new rules. Courts are an obvious example. Other types of referees are also needed to regulate, monitor, and document the various kinds of transactions taking place: tax authorities, accountants, lawyers, and on and on. That is, the process of returning to a market economy also required a fundamental change in how the government worked, often referred to as "state-building" or "institutional reform." Russia was trying to do all of this while the Communist Party that had ruled the country for 70 years had collapsed and the Soviet Union itself had disintegrated.

It is therefore not surprising that many mistakes were made. Thinking about the Russian economic reform process in the 1990s as primarily an issue of mistakes and who made them, however, is the wrong way to think about it. Every post-communist country, no matter how quickly or slowly it reformed, went through a recession—the question was how long and severe the recession was. In Russia official GDP dropped by 40 percent from 1990 to 1998, although this overstates the decline because Soviet official GDP numbers were artificially inflated, including useless and even fake activity. Other measures of economic activity also fell, such as the amount of electricity used or the amount of retail trade, but not as severely as the GDP figures.

Economic depression was accompanied by several years of hyperinflation. As hard as it may be to believe, inflation was over 2,500 percent in 1992 and 800 percent in 1993, dropping to "only" 215 percent in 1994. This hyperinflation was a consequence both of freeing prices that had been kept artificially low for literally decades and a complete failure to control the money supply. The latter task was not even possible because it was not until mid-1993 that Russia had its own currency and a central bank that solely controlled its emission and circulation; prior to that, most of the other former Soviet republics also continued to use the ruble.

For many people the economic shock was severe. Economic disorder contributed to a sharp spike in mortality, and life expectancy in the early 1990s dropped from 74 to 71 for females and from 64 to 58 for males. At the same time, the economic situation in Russia was more or less average compared to its post-Soviet peers—in fact, of the 15 former Soviet republics, half did worse than Russia in terms of change in GDP per capita as of 2000, and half did better. In other words, this is not so much a Russia story as it is a story about the consequences of the implosion of communism throughout the entire region.

An alternative and more useful way to think about Russian economic performance after the Soviet collapse is to think not about choices and mistakes but about conditions and circumstances. The most important condition was the breakdown of the country and its political and economic system. After more than 75 years of Communist Party rule and more than 60 years of a communist economy, Russia was trying to start over as a new country. Trade and supply links within the Soviet Union and the communist bloc broke down. Many of the most basic institutions needed to run a modern economy were either nonexistent or extremely weak. Much of Russia's economic inheritance was unsuited for capitalist economic competition, including factories that were too large, technologically outdated, located in cold and remote areas, and, in the words of one economist, "almost comically inefficient" in their use of resources. Yet closing uncompetitive factories wholesale was not a realistic option either,

5. A Russian soldier gives money to an old woman begging on Red Square in 1998. Economic inequality increased sharply in post-Soviet Russia.

given the massive human costs that would follow, such as mass unemployment—which in turn would have had severe political costs for government officials at all levels.

Politically, Russia was also at a disadvantage compared with most other post-communist states. In places like Estonia, Poland, and

Hungary, there was national pride about breaking free from Soviet domination and enthusiasm about a "return to Europe," with the realistic prospect of joining the European Union if far-reaching economic reforms were implemented. Russia, in contrast, was politically divided about the Soviet collapse and the economic path forward. Throughout the 1990s there was persistent and rancorous political confrontation between President Boris Yeltsin, who was rhetorically committed to rapid economic reform, and opposition political parties that strongly rejected this project.

Last but certainly not least, world energy prices were at very low levels in the 1990s, spelling hardship for Russia's oil- and gas-dependent economy. During Yeltsin's presidency, the average price of a barrel of oil was less than 18 dollars; for comparison, over the next 15 years the average price was more than 3.5 times higher. Indeed, one economist estimated that most of Russia's economic growth from 2000 to 2015 can be explained by changes in world oil prices.

If the political causes of economic performance were overstated, due more to communist legacies, geography, and resource wealth than to policy choices, the political consequences of changing economic growth rates were substantial. The Russian public blamed Yeltsin for a decade of economic depression and social instability, giving him single-digit approval ratings by the end of his presidency. In 1999 the opposition-controlled parliament tried to impeach Yeltsin for, among other things, "the genocide of the Russian people." In contrast, eight years of solid economic growth, rising living standards, and perceptions of greater stability drove Putin's approval rating to a high of 87 percent by December 2007. Although Russia's economic performance since 2014 has been considerably worse, with average growth of less than 1 percent per year between 2014 and 2022, the specter of a return to the "rough '90s" still helps generate political support for Putin.

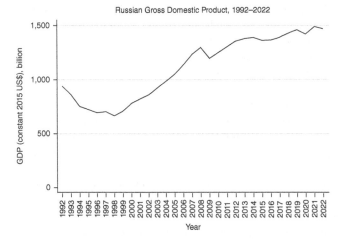

Russian Gross Domestic Product, 1992–2022

6. **Graph of Russian economic performance from 1992 to 2022. Data are adjusted to control for inflation and show the value of Russian gross domestic product in 2015 US dollars.**

The politics of Russia's new economy

Russia's "economic transition" is long since over. There are no five-year plans telling factories what to produce, much of the economy is now in private hands, and consumers are overwhelmed with goods and services rather than queueing for basic necessities. Like consumers elsewhere in much of the world, urban shoppers in Russia can go to the mall or the supermarket or online when they need something, and they use apps on their smartphones to order a taxi or food delivery. Life is not necessarily easier for everyone, but daily economic life for urban Russians looks much like it would in other countries at similar income levels.

GDP per capita provides a rough comparative measure of people's living standards across countries, especially when using estimates that adjust for different price levels across countries. As of 2020,

Russia ranked 50th in the world, with a GDP per capita of about $29,000. Russians' standard of living was thus roughly comparable to Turkey, Malaysia, or Croatia, and about 45 percent of that in the United States. Russian GDP per capita was well ahead of China (about $17,000).

These national averages obviously obscure significant regional differences across Russia's vast territory. The standard of living in Moscow is not that different from many other European cities. In contrast, Russia's poorest regions are more comparable to Central America or South Asia in terms of living standards. More than 20 percent of Russian households are not connected to centralized sewer systems, including two-thirds of those in rural areas. Russian economic geographers describe sharp differences between large cities with good economic prospects, struggling smaller cities with declining prospects unless close to a major city, and small towns and rural areas where the population is shrinking and economic prospects are poor.

But there are several features of Russia's economy that are distinctive and have important political implications. First, Russia's economy is heavily dependent on natural resource exports, especially oil and gas. It is one of the top three world producers of both oil and gas and a top ten producer of coal. Fossil fuels typically represent more than 60 percent of Russia's export earnings, and oil and gas revenues tend to make up 35 to 50 percent of federal budget revenues. Between 10 and 25 percent of Russia's GDP comes from hydrocarbons. Six of Russia's seven largest companies are energy companies, including the top five. State-owned enterprises are responsible for the majority of Russia's oil and gas production.

Second, the state plays a sizable role in the Russian economy. According to a former advisor to President Putin, Putin believes that "there should be maximum oneness of state and business." State banks account for more than half of the entire banking sector. Besides energy and finance, the state also plays a big role in such sectors as transport, aviation, and machinery. Half of people's incomes in Russia come from the state in one way or another, whether it be from pensions or state-sector wages. The flip side of this issue is that small private companies, traditional drivers of innovation, play a lesser role in the Russian economy than in many of its peers.

Third, inequality in Russia is high. This is a sharp reversal from the communist period—although Communist Party insiders had access to elite apartments and special stores, they did not have massive wealth to pass on to their children. Today, the 500 Russians who are worth more than $100 million, according to one study, collectively own $640 billion, 40 percent of the entire country's household wealth. Another economic study determined that "there is as much financial wealth held by rich Russians abroad . . . as held by the entire Russian population in Russia itself." One Swiss bank concluded that Russia is the world's most unequal large economy. Russia's ultra-rich became famous in the 1990s as the so-called oligarchs, known for their expensive taste and political influence. One of Putin's main priorities as president was bringing the oligarchs to heel and ensuring their loyalty to the state, and he put acquaintances in charge of some of the most important companies. The politically subordinate status of Russia's ultra-rich is captured by the Russian joke that there are no billionaires in Russia, only people working as billionaires.

These three features of the Russian economy—dependence on oil and gas, a large state role in the economy, and high inequality— are interconnected and influence Russian politics. Collectively, they help maintain an authoritarian political system and impede Russia's further economic modernization. According to some experts, Russia today has the kind of economy we should expect. Its economic advantage is rooted in its natural resources—not only oil, gas, and coal but also timber, diamonds, and metals such as aluminum, nickel, and copper. It makes sense for Russia to export these resources, as well as commodities such as grain, and use the money to buy finished goods like computers and clothes. Moreover, natural resource income helps prop up the inefficient parts of the Russian economy left over from the Soviet period that it would be politically costly to get rid of, such as industrial enterprises that were established in remote and cold areas under Stalin. Given these conditions, the nature of the Russian economy and political system is unlikely to change.

Other experts disagree. They believe that with a different economic strategy, Russia could join the world's top economies, or at least make up some of the ground on them, something that it has been unable to do for the past several hundred years. This new strategy would try to take advantage of Russia's highly educated society to boost innovation, entrepreneurship, and productivity, and thereby move the Russian economy away from resource dependency and toward a twenty-first-century knowledge-based economy. As things stand today, Russia is not innovative and productive enough to compete with the world's richest countries in cutting-edge economic sectors, and its wages and production costs are too high to be competitive with lower-income developing countries. Political repression and resistance to the Russo-Ukraine War also contribute to brain drain, with talented young people leaving the country.

Are Russia's political leaders interested in moving away from resource dependence and toward a more diverse and innovative economy? At least rhetorically, top Russian politicians have talked about weaning the economy off the addiction to the "oil needle." Dmitriy Medvedev, a close Putin ally who was president from 2008 to 2012, talked frequently about the need for economic modernization. He argued that Russia was stuck in a "middle-income trap" and needed to improve the business climate to increase investment and raise productivity.

For the most part, however, the Russian authorities in general, and President Putin in particular, have not been interested in pursuing this alternative approach to economic development. Although when he first became president Putin wanted Russia to catch up to European countries like Portugal or Spain in terms of level of development and personal income, that goal has fallen by the wayside as economic growth has slowed to a crawl.

A far-reaching economic development strategy would require fundamental changes in how Russia works. Currently, Russia ranks in the bottom half of the world in terms of controlling corruption, the rule of law, the quality of regulations, and the accountability of the government. It does a poor job of protecting property rights. In other words, its political, economic, and legal institutions are too low quality for Russia to achieve high levels of growth based on boosting domestic and foreign investment and increasing productivity.

Take the example of property rights. A functioning market economy needs rules about who owns what and what they can do with their property, and these rules need to be enforced in a generally fair way. At the individual level, most Russians acquired ownership of their apartment or house after the Soviet collapse in the 1990s—for free. This was a very big deal and something many Russians simply take for granted. Some people were swindled out of their housing during this change, but for most people the current housing market works more efficiently than the interminable waiting lists of the Soviet period.

For businesses, the challenges are more severe. In the early days of the transition to capitalism, mafia-type organizations sprung up to run protection rackets that demanded payments from small businesses. Big businesses created their own robust private security forces and hired former law enforcement officers to smooth relations with their former colleagues still working for the state. The very state bodies that are supposed to protect the property rights of businesses—police, prosecutors, and courts— got involved in corrupt schemes to extort private businesses. The Russian sociologist Vadim Volkov observed that the small-time bandit was driven out by state employees behaving like bandits. Law enforcement agencies even battle with each other over who gets to oversee, and thus profit from, illegal activities such as money laundering.

The Russian journalist Maxim Trudolyubov posited a rough rule of thumb about the relationship between the state and business: "The larger and more important an asset is, the more conditional is the right to own it." The state expects the owners of the largest businesses to advance state goals, such as paying for facilities for the 2014 Sochi Winter Olympics, even if the business will take a loss on the venture. Russia's billionaire oligarchs, both those who were major oligarchs before Putin came to power and those who became billionaires because they were connected to Putin, have stressed their willingness to turn over their companies to the state if the state asks. "If you control the chief economic assets," said one former state security officer, "then you are essentially holding everyone by the balls." Trudolyubov argues that the best way for businesses in Russia to succeed is not to be more entrepreneurial and bring in more profits and investment, but to seek privileges and protection from the state.

Changing how the economy works would take real political commitment and would also have real political consequences. To raise productivity, stimulate entrepreneurship, and increase investment from domestic and foreign sources, Russia would need stronger protection of property rights, lower state corruption, and a greater commitment to the rule of law. In most cases, building better economic and legal institutions requires a political environment in which the media can report openly on corruption (meaning the use of public office for private gain) and malfeasance, and opposition political parties can criticize the government. That is, good economic governance in high-income countries usually goes together with democracy. That is why those economic experts who think Russia could move up into the group of wealthier world countries tend to think this can only happen with economic and political reforms. From the point of view of Putin and many of Russia's political and economic elites, however, an economy in which oil and gas dominate and the state plays a large role is safer and more stable than one in which the government tries to carry out major reforms in how the political and economic system works. These politically connected elites are also able to grow massively wealthy, living extravagant lifestyles unimaginable to average Russians—another reason they oppose political reforms that would help tackle corruption.

The war against Ukraine has set back Russia's future economic development even further. Many countries introduced harsh sanctions against the Russian economy that will limit future growth, and thousands of global companies cut back or severed their relationships with Russia. Russian GDP plunged once again in 2022, despite high world energy prices. The economy rebounded the following year after the initial shock, but this growth was driven entirely by war spending. The wartime economic model is a step backward that further delays a possible transition to a more globally competitive economic model. Putin declared at the beginning of his rule that foreign investment and global economic integration were vital for Russia's economic progress. His aggressive foreign policy has closed the door on that trajectory.

Changes in European energy habits could have a major and negative effect on the Russian economy. The European Union is transitioning away from Russian hydrocarbons, due both to climate change and the Russo-Ukraine War. Prior to the war, 50 to 60 percent of Russia's oil exports and 75 percent of its natural gas exports went to Europe. Because of the war, the EU rapidly reduced Russian fossil fuel imports. The global shift away from hydrocarbons due to climate change represents a serious challenge to Russia's economic model over the past five decades. The economic consequences of the war mean that this day of reckoning could come even sooner.

The economic changes since the death of communism have radically remade Russian society. Most people own their own homes or apartments. If half of the people's incomes come from the state, that means that half comes from private sources—also a stark change from the Soviet era. Gray urban environments with little consumer choice were transformed into bright and lively twenty-first-century cities with the coffee shops, tattoo parlors, vegetarian restaurants, and whiskey bars to match, especially in Moscow and Saint Petersburg. A major political question is whether the Russian people will be satisfied with continued economic stagnation, declining living standards, high inequality, and a partial return to economic isolation. Although the economy became more open, the political system, after a brief opening, remains closed.

Chapter 4

The failed experiment of democratic constitutionalism

The Russian human rights lawyer Marina Agaltsova arrived in the United States in 2018 for a conference on the Russian Constitution. The border control agent was confused. "A constitution? You have a constitution?" he asked. "I thought you just had Mr. Putin."

Russia has a constitution. The first article of the Russian Constitution declares that Russia is a "democratic, federal, rule-of-law state." The second article maintains that "human rights and freedoms are the highest value." Neither of those claims is true. Today, Russia is an authoritarian state in which the principles of federalism and the rule of law are frequently ignored, and human rights are often disregarded or repressed.

On the other hand, Russia does have some political features that *look* democratic. There are elections, including for president and for most regional governors. There is a Constitutional Court. There are elected legislatures at the national, regional, and local levels. Sometimes there are even electoral surprises, especially at the regional and local level. That said, President Vladimir Putin and his ruling United Russia party have a firm grip on power.

Political scientists call this type of government "electoral authoritarianism"—an authoritarian regime inside a democratic shell.

Electoral authoritarianism is not some Russian aberration. In fact, according to one major research project assessing government types around the world (V-Dem), there were 60 electoral authoritarian countries in 2021, making it the most common type of political system in the world. Historically speaking, authoritarianism of one form or another is also very common—it is democracy that has been the greater anomaly until relatively recently.

There was a brief period, however, when it seemed that Russia might become a successful democracy. In the summer of 1989, the political scientist Francis Fukuyama famously stated, "We may be witnessing not just the end of the Cold War . . , [but] the universalization of Western liberal democracy as the final form of human government." A few months later the Berlin Wall fell, and a couple of years after that the Soviet Union itself collapsed. Russia's new leader, Boris Yeltsin, declared before a joint session of the US Congress in June 1992 that Russia had "made its choice in favor of liberty and democracy."

Russia's democratization in the early 1990s coincided with trends elsewhere in the region and the world. As Fukuyama noted, at that time democracy was more and more seen as the most natural and appropriate form of government. Democracy spread around the globe, encompassing governments on all continents, including places that previously were supposedly prone to authoritarianism. Some of those countries that democratized between the 1970s and the 2000s have remained democratic. Others, including Russia, have not. Russia has an authoritarian political system, at least for now.

The authoritarian past

For centuries the dominant political order in Russia has been autocratic. Democratic principles of constitutional government and liberal ideas about freedom, rights, and the rule of law began to develop and spread in Europe and North America in the seventeenth century. Russia's tsars naturally resisted such ideas, connecting their mandate to rule to divine right. Factors such as Russia's challenging geography and climate, intense geopolitical competition with powerful European neighbors, predominantly peasant society, and a desire to "catch up" with the leading industrial economies further reinforced state primacy and autocratic rule.

Yet ideas about democratic rule and constitutional government spread to Russia as well. The Russian Revolution of 1905–1906 failed to unseat Tsar Nicholas II, but it did force him to issue Russia's first constitution in 1906. That constitution created Russia's first modern parliament, the Duma. In principle, the constitution offered the possibility of putting constraints on the autocrats' heretofore unlimited power and moving Russia in the direction of a state constrained by law. In reality, however, Nicholas II and the state bureaucracy were opposed to meaningful limits on their power, and the regime was overthrown in 1917.

The Communist Party of the Soviet Union (CPSU) built a completely different type of authoritarian political order. Members of the Soviet political leadership based their right to rule not on a mandate from God (monarchy) or the people (democracy), but on their belief that Marxist-Leninist ideology had uncovered the laws of history and that it was their mission to build and spread socialism. The CPSU was the ultimate source of legitimate authority. This was reflected in the design of political institutions. The CPSU was not a political party comparable to political parties in democratic states; it did not compete with other parties for the right to hold political office and govern the country. Rather, it was the only legal political party, and it established parallel structures at all levels of government to monitor and control the state. The Soviet Union is one of the first and most prominent examples of what political scientists call a single-party or one-party political system. The centrality of party rule to the Soviet system was made most explicit in the 1977 constitution, which stated that the Communist Party was "[t]he leading and guiding force of Soviet society and the nucleus of its political system, of all state organizations and public organizations."

Despite the radically different political systems, tsarist Russia and the Soviet Union shared one thing in common: the primacy of the state. In particular, the state's central executive did not recognize or submit to meaningful constraints from other government bodies (legislatures, courts, or subnational regional governments), from a constitution or other laws, or from the people. Soviet leader Mikhail Gorbachev thus made a bold departure from historical precedent when he announced in 1988 that the Soviet Union would have competitive national elections in 1989 for a new parliament called the Congress of People's Deputies. The following year Gorbachev removed the constitutional provision on the "leading and guiding role" of the CPSU and inserted a president into the system, although he had the Congress of People's Deputies select him as president rather than submitting to a popular election.

Gorbachev served as president for less than two years before the Soviet Union dissolved. But his creation of a Soviet presidency paved the way for Russia to adopt a presidential system of government. Gorbachev's advisors explicitly drew on Western models—in particular, those of the United States and France—when designing the new Soviet presidency. Most of the 15 Soviet republics, including Russia, followed suit and also created the position of president. Boris Yeltsin was elected president of the

Russian Federation inside the Soviet Union in June 1991 with 57 percent of the vote in a fair democratic election. Yeltsin, therefore, had popular legitimacy in a way that Gorbachev did not, even though Yeltsin's status was only as leader of one republic inside the USSR. When the Soviet Union collapsed in December 1991, Gorbachev lost his presidency and his country, and Yeltsin moved into the Kremlin as president of a newly independent Russia.

Russia's democratic choice?

Russia entered independent statehood in January 1992 facing multiple crises. The Soviet Union had just splintered into 15 separate states, and there were serious fears about the future territorial integrity of Russia. The government's key priority was economic—the country was broke, and the economic system was broken. The political system, if not completely broken, was also undergoing a serious crisis. President Yeltsin had banned the CPSU after a failed hardliner coup attempt in August 1991 that tried to overthrow Gorbachev. The KGB (Committee on State Security) director had been the chief organizer of the coup attempt, which led Yeltsin to split the powerful secret police agency into five separate parts. The extant constitution, adopted in 1978, had been heavily amended in recent years, making it internally contradictory on some crucial issues. Rather than trying to adopt a new constitution and call new presidential and legislative elections, Yeltsin decided that economic reform was the priority. A constitutional commission began debating the parameters of a new constitution in 1990, and these discussions continued in 1992 and 1993.

Russia was undergoing a revolutionary transformation across multiple dimensions. Starting with President Yeltsin and going down to the average person on the street, Russians asked: What are the boundaries of our state? How do we turn a communist economic system into a capitalist one? How do we turn an authoritarian one-party state into a democratic one, and what should be the rules of a new democratic order? On all of these questions, there was no elite and mass consensus on the answers. Russian politics was sharply polarized.

In September and October 1993 this polarization turned deadly. On one side was President Yeltsin; on the other, the Congress of People's Deputies and Yeltsin's own vice president, who sided with the Congress. Both sides violated the constitution and used violence during the showdown. After the Congress's armed supporters tried to seize the capital's television tower on the night of October 3, Yeltsin called on the army and security services to storm the parliament building the next day. Yeltsin's former vice president, the parliamentary speaker, and other key opponents of Yeltsin were arrested. Over two days of violence in Moscow, 147 people died. The October 1993 events were a stark indication of the fragility of Russia's political institutions. Having dispersed the parliament, Yeltsin was now in a position to impose a constitution of his choosing. Voters approved the new constitution in a national referendum in December 1993.

The new Russian Constitution was a radical departure from all previous Russian and Soviet constitutions in two important ways. First, it put a strong emphasis on the rights and freedoms of the people. Article 3 states that "the sole source of power in the Russian Federation is its multinational people." The section on "the rights and freedoms of the person and the citizen" comes before the sections describing the distribution of power among the different branches of government. The rights enumerated in the constitution include freedom of conscience and religion, assembly, association, and privacy, as well as other rights related to legal and criminal matters, such as the right to a trial, presumption of innocence, protection from torture, and the right to private property. It also includes a variety of social and economic rights, such as healthcare, social security, and education. Importantly, international legal norms and treaties adopted by Russia were part of domestic law and had priority over domestic law if they were in conflict (this provision was largely overturned by a 2020 constitutional revision).

A second important departure from past constitutions was the design of political institutions based on checks and balances and the separation of powers. At the federal level, it established a bicameral parliament, the Federal Assembly, composed of a State Duma of 450 elected members and a Federation Council with two representatives for each region (currently 89, according to Russian law, which includes six regions illegally seized from Ukraine). The executive branch has two parts: a directly elected president and a prime minister who heads what Russians call the government (the ministries and other executive branch agencies). This design is technically "semi-presidential," like that in France. Finally, there is a Constitutional Court with the power of judicial review, or the ability to declare acts of the executive and legislative branches unconstitutional.

The separation of powers in the 1993 constitution is not only horizontal—across the different branches of government at the national level—but also vertical, meaning a federal system. Each region has its own legislature and executive branch, headed by a governor—or in three cases a mayor (in the "federal cities" of Moscow, Saint Petersburg, and Sevastopol, the capital of the illegally annexed region of Crimea). Local self-government is also stated as a core constitutional principle.

On paper, then, Russia was entering a new period in its history: the creation of a democratic political order in which citizens had extensive rights and the various branches of government would check and balance each other, thereby insuring the stability and longevity of Russia's democracy. The drafters of the new constitution drew extensively on foreign examples, as Russia aspired to become a liberal democracy, which at the time of adoption in 1993 was considered the "normal" path of political development for many countries around the world. However, democratic constitutionalism has failed in Russia—at least so far.

What explains this failure? There are multiple reasons, but no scholarly consensus on which are the most important. Some would argue that the project was doomed from the beginning. First of all, the very origins of the new Russia were unpromising. Russia had no meaningful democratic history and was born out of the chaotic collapse of communism and empire. The new constitution was imposed from above by a president who had won a violent struggle for power, not based on a political compromise between rival political forces. Although some of these contending groups seemed genuinely committed to forging a democratic system, the commitment of others was in doubt, and some were actively hostile to it.

Second, the parameters of the constitutional document itself are a problem. In particular, it gives too much power to the president. What looks like French-style semi-presidentialism on paper is really more super-presidential. The president has extensive decree powers (true of some other presidential systems as well), which Yeltsin used to implement major economic changes without legislative approval. The prime minister has relatively weak powers. Moreover, the president ultimately has the power to dismiss the Duma if it rejects his or her nominee for prime minister, which means that whoever becomes prime minister is heavily dependent on the president. So far there have been only two exceptions to this pattern. First, for six months in 1998–1999, Yeltsin had to accept a prime minister favored by the Duma because of his weak position after the 1998 global financial crisis. Second, from 2008 to 2012, Putin served as prime minister because of a former constitutional provision limiting him to two consecutive terms as president. Yet everyone knew that for those four years President Dmitriy Medvedev was at least as dependent on Prime Minister Putin as Putin was on him. Arguably, the most consequential thing that Medvedev did as president was to amend the constitution to increase presidential terms from four to six years, a provision so far used only by Vladimir Putin

(Medvedev also increased terms for Duma members from four to five years).

The constitution was problematic in other ways as well. For example, it was vague about how the Federation Council—the branch of parliament based on the federal principle of two members per region (often referred to as "senators," based on the American example)—is formed. The constitution stipulates that one senator per region comes from the regional executive and one from the regional legislature, which seems to imply they are not elected directly by the citizens. For a while the governor of each region was also a senator in the Federation Council, making each of them both a legislator at the national level and the chief executive at the subnational level. That proved unworkable in practice, and these posts have become de facto appointed by the president, which undermines both the principle of separation of powers and the principle of federalism. The constitutional article stating that there is "a unified system of executive power" in the country also seems at odds with the core principle of federalism.

In general, Russia's 1993 constitution borrowed considerably from foreign models and included many of the institutional design features found in constitutional democracies. At the same time, there were also passages rooted in Russian traditions that prioritize the primacy of the state and its central executive. It undeniably was more democratic on paper than previous Russian and Soviet constitutions, but would that be enough?

Yeltsin's ambiguous legacy

No written document—what political scientists sometimes call a "parchment institutions"—can enforce itself. Despite the problems of the origins and design of the 1993 constitution, it is too deterministic to say it was doomed to fail. The document was flawed, but probably not fatally so. Rather, we should look to politics and politicians to explain why the constitution was unable to sustain Russian democracy.

When Yeltsin unexpectedly resigned the presidency on December 31, 1999, he asked Russians for their forgiveness. He apologized for people's suffering, for the mistakes he had made, for his failures, and for his naiveté. "Many of our dreams did not come true," he lamented. He falsely believed, he said, that Russia could "in one great leap jump from a gray, stagnant, totalitarian past into a radiant, rich, civilized future." Yeltsin was mostly talking about economic difficulties, not political ones. Indeed, he took credit for "creating a most important precedent of a civilized, voluntary transfer of power" from one elected president to another. "Russia," he declared, "will never return to the past."

Yeltsin was correct that leaving office voluntarily was a very important precedent. Indeed, he is the only Russian ruler ever to voluntarily give up power. His successor, Vladimir Putin, in contrast, has gone to great lengths to remain in power far beyond his two initial terms as president. In that sense, Russia has returned to the past quite quickly. Even Yeltsin's departure, however, was an ambiguous achievement. He gave up his power, but he could have served out his term and let a competitive election take place on the normal schedule. Instead, Yeltsin's early resignation was designed to give Putin the status of acting president at a time when his popularity was peaking, thus making it highly likely that Putin would win. He won in the first round with 53 percent of the vote in his first bid for public office at any level. It was the most democratic election of his career.

Other parts of Yeltsin's legacy with respect to Russia's political regime—the extent to which it is democratic or authoritarian—are equally ambiguous. On the positive side, Russian elections in the 1990s were generally democratic and competitive. They were democratic in the most basic sense that they took place according to regular procedures, the ballots were in most cases counted fairly, and there was genuine uncertainty about the results. Opposition parties dominated the Duma throughout the Yeltsin era, and efforts to create a strong pro-Yeltsin political party were feeble. Elections at the regional and local level were a mixed bag: they were generally democratic and competitive in some places, but more authoritarian and controlled in others. There are also genuine doubts about whether Yeltsin would have conceded power if he had lost the 1996 presidential election. Some of his closest advisers nearly persuaded him to cancel the election. Fearing the consequences of a communist victory, the main oligarchs (wealthy, politically powerful businessmen) rallied to Yeltsin's side, delivering slanted coverage on the main television channels and pouring money into his campaign well above the legal limit. In some regions there were clear signs of pro-Yeltsin ballot stuffing, although generally the counting appears to have been fair.

In addition, essential aspects of a democratic political system, such as free speech, a free media, and the right to organize in opposition to the state, were generally upheld. The state did not throw people in jail or harass them for criticizing Yeltsin or his close associates. There was genuine political pluralism in the 1990s in Russia. On balance, Russia was an electoral democracy, albeit deeply flawed. An electoral democracy is one in which elections are generally free and fair and political rights are generally respected, yet there are also major deficits in such areas as the rule of law and control of corruption. To some observers, the flaws in the constitution and Yeltsin's rule were so extensive that it should not even count as a democracy.

Yeltsin's Russia did have big problems. The privatization of Soviet state property helped create a small group of oligarchs who had a disproportionate influence on politics. Oligarchs sought to control loyal media outlets, cut deals with parties and politicians to protect their business interests, and manipulated the law enforcement system to help themselves and hurt their rivals. These practices helped weaken the rule of law and convinced many average Russians that politics was a dirty elite game that thwarted the will and interests of average citizens. The war in Chechnya led to massive human rights violations and empowered security and military officials inside the state. Rising crime and economic dislocation contributed to a sense that the state was in crisis and failing the population. By the time Yeltsin dramatically resigned, his approval ratings were in single digits and people were ready for a new ruler.

Putin's options

Yeltsin chose Putin as his prime minister in August 1999 and resigned four months later in order to pave the way to a Putin presidency, primarily because he valued Putin's loyalty. Yeltsin had appreciated Putin's competence and low-key demeanor in several important posts in the late 1990s. He also thought Putin had the right profile for the times. Yeltsin claimed society was looking for a leader who was both a "new-thinking democrat" and a "strong, military man," and he thought Putin fit the bill.

In a major statement on the eve of his presidency, Putin extolled "the benefits of democracy, a law-governed state, and individual and political freedom." Yet Russia has become steadily less democratic and more authoritarian during Putin's reign. Did Putin have a plan to build authoritarianism from the beginning, or did he move in that direction as a response to circumstances? Regardless of Putin's ideas and ambitions, important features of Russia's political institutions and circumstances made his authoritarian turn possible.

Putin took power at a time of perceived crisis for the Russian state. Western journalists openly questioned whether Russia was "another Somalia" or a "failed state." Russia had defaulted on its debts in 1998 because of the global financial crisis and had trouble collecting taxes and upholding the ruble as the national currency in the face of widespread barter and surrogate monies. Some

7. President Boris Yeltsin leaves the Kremlin on December 31, 1999, after resigning and handing power to Prime Minister Vladimir Putin (front left).

observers feared a loss of central control of the military and other state coercive agencies. Yeltsin was ailing and had lost public support. At the personal level, Putin presented a sharp contrast with the frail and aging Yeltsin: young (48 at the time), physically active, abstemious, and a former lieutenant colonel in the KGB.

Putin's top priority in his first years was confronting this perceived crisis of the central state. He was determined to restore what he called "vertical power" and assert the central government's dominance over the regions. He wanted to weaken the political influence of the oligarchs, vowing that he would end "the fusion of power and capital." Two oligarchs who controlled major television channels were his first targets, and they were forced to flee the country. Putin wanted to build a pro-government majority in the parliament to adopt his legislative agenda. Finally, he wanted to regain central state control over state security, and over law

enforcement organs and the legal system more generally, believing
that the regions had too much sway in this realm.

The Russian Constitution gave Putin important tools to consolidate
his power. Yeltsin had been largely unable to use these tools. In the
aftermath of the Soviet collapse, Yeltsin faced a collapsing economy,
a very weak state, parliamentary opposition, and a dissatisfied
population. He also suffered from health problems. Putin came
to power at the time the economy was starting to recover and with
high popularity due to the resumption of the Chechen War. He was
better positioned to make super-presidentialism a reality.

Building a super-presidential order had the consequence of fatally
weakening Russia's fragile democratic institutions. Taking control
over the main television channels meant that competing oligarchic
channels were replaced with pro-Putin messaging that
marginalized dissenting voices. Yeltsin-era oligarchs who wanted
to keep their riches had to fall in line with the Kremlin on political
matters and contribute to Kremlin priorities. Regional governors
had to cut back their national political profiles, and in 2004 Putin
announced that these positions would be appointed and not
elected (they became elected again after 2012, but with Kremlin
control over who could run). Electoral rules were repeatedly
changed to benefit Putin's political party, United Russia.

By 2005, shortly after Putin's second term began, the democracy-
rating organization Freedom House no longer considered Russia
an electoral democracy. It had crossed over the admittedly blurry
line between democracy and authoritarianism. The key difference
is that in a democracy the opposition can win elections, whereas
in an electoral authoritarian regime the elections are so unfair
and so tilted in favor of the ruling group that the opposition
has almost no chance of winning. Russia has become increasingly
authoritarian under Putin, and presidential power has become
even stronger—a move from super-presidentialism to
hyper-presidentialism.

The nature of Russian authoritarianism

Political scientists categorize authoritarian regimes based on two different factors: the degree of authoritarianism and the type of authoritarianism. Russia is considered an electoral authoritarian regime due to holding periodic (albeit unfair) elections for a variety of public offices at different levels of government, including the presidency and the Duma. Over time, Russian electoral authoritarianism has become increasingly uncompetitive. The ruling United Russia party takes a large majority of the Duma seats and almost all the regional governorships. The seats that do not go to United Russia go to other parties—such as the Communist Party and the misleadingly named Liberal Democratic Party—that tend to cooperate with the Kremlin on all important issues, what Russians call the "systemic opposition." Real opposition parties are prevented from competing. Presidential elections since 2004 have been more like coronations, with an average gap between the winner and the second-place candidate of more than 50 percentage points. In 2020 Putin changed the 1993 constitution in important ways that further strengthened the presidency. Most importantly, the new constitution "nullified" Putin's prior presidential terms, thereby allowing him to run for president two more times and potentially stay in power for more than 36 years. He was "re-elected" (the process was more like a coronation than an actual election) to a fifth term in March 2024, and he can run again in 2030.

There are four basic types of contemporary authoritarianism: monarchies, military regimes, single-party regimes, and personalist dictatorships. Russia's form of electoral authoritarianism is closest to the personalist dictatorship type. In personalist regimes like Putin's, the leader is relatively unencumbered by either countervailing institutions or groups of elites. Saying that Russia is a personalist authoritarian regime does not mean that Putin decides everything on his own or that there are no other powerful elites. However, Putin can usually have the final word on policy issues that are important to him.

The US border control agent, then, had a point when he wondered why Russia needed a constitution when it had Putin. In personalist regimes, the formal institutions of government—constitutions, rules, laws, courts, legislatures, and so on—are a weak and bendable constraint on the ruler. In an electoral authoritarian regime, it is important that the government pretend to follow the rules to uphold the fiction that it is a democracy, but real politics is driven more by what the ruler wants than what the rules say.

The paradox of personalist regimes is that the strength of the ruler actually makes formal government institutions weaker. Putin and other personalist rulers like him have been called "weak strongmen." Personalist rulers face three core problems. First, institutions are weak. This is a problem because even personalist leaders rely on these institutions to get things done and carry out decisions. Second, there are complex trade-offs between keeping elites happy and keeping average citizens happy. With the official procedures for leadership change (elections) disabled, personalist rulers must fear threats from both the elites (coups) and the streets (revolution). Third, the ruler has to balance, in the words of Italian political philosopher Niccolò Machiavelli, love and fear. Authoritarian leaders want to be popular, and so they must seek support by delivering things that people want, such as economic prosperity or foreign policy success, and by shaping the information citizens receive through the media. Yet authoritarian leaders also need the ability to repress and intimidate potential challengers. Machiavelli thought it is best to be both feared and loved, but that if a ruler has to choose, it is safer to be feared than loved.

All three of these things have been problems in Russia. For example, decision-making procedures are often chaotic and inefficient. Some decisions are unnecessarily delayed as officials try to figure out what Putin might want, or those on the losing end try to appeal to "the boss" to side with them. Other decisions are adopted not through coherent procedures but because someone close to Putin, or perceived as close, can steer decisions in their favor. If the policy area is not a priority for Putin, inactivity is often the default outcome. The Duma, rather than being an independent source of legislation and policy ideas, often either serves as a rubber-stamp for Kremlin initiatives or becomes an arena in which parts of the executive branch bureaucracy battle each other for power and resources. Judges, rather than applying the law, sometimes decide cases based on what they assume the Kremlin wants, or even under direct political influence.

The Russian government often struggles to successfully implement decisions it has taken. Since the late 2000s, Putin has routinely announced a series of national strategies, decrees, and programs designed to improve a variety of core state tasks, from education to healthcare to infrastructure. One reform program replaces another, with the results generally falling well short of the initial ambitious goals. The weakness of government institutions puts Russia on a treadmill of reforms, with lots of activity but not much forward progress. Russia frequently performs poorly compared with other comparable countries in such indicators of government performance as corruption, the rule of law, government transparency, judicial independence, personal safety, and environmental protection.

A key issue for the Russian state, like other contemporary authoritarian regimes, has been how much to rely on repression versus persuasion. The Russian economist Sergei Guriev and the American political scientist Daniel Treisman refer to Russia as an "information autocracy" and Putin as a "spin dictator." By controlling information, rulers like Putin can achieve authoritarian control without using the more brutal methods of past dictators. Control over television was an early and top priority for Putin, even though he allowed more freedom in print and online media. As the Internet has grown in importance, efforts of the Russian government to control that space have increased. The Kremlin also carefully tracks public opinion and changes its messaging—and occasionally its actual policies—to show responsiveness to the public will.

More generally, Russian authoritarianism in its hyper-presidentialist and personalist form depends on the notion that there is no alternative to the current ruler. State television propaganda emphasizes Putin's achievements and does not give access to opponents who might criticize him or his policies. The CEO of the top state television channel has stated openly that his main job is to mobilize and consolidate the country, and that informing people about what is going on is a secondary task. Elections, similarly, are tilted in favor of the president and the United Russia party. Genuine opponents are kept off the ballot. The result of this form of control is that no obvious alternatives to Putin are allowed to break through and gain wide popularity. This kind of personalist regime is made to seem inevitable, with no other options available.

Spin is important, but so is repression. This repression is often low-intensity—surveillance, harassment, bogus criminal cases, forbidding opposition protests and dispersing "illegal" protests with minimal violence, refusal to register opposition parties and nongovernmental organizations (NGOs), and so on. The state argues that it is only upholding the law, and the courts—as part of the state—go along. Over time, repression has been ratcheted up, with opposition-minded organizations and individuals facing restrictions and bans. High-intensity repression—shooting protestors, death squads, mass killings—has generally been avoided, although the state tried to poison prominent opposition figure Aleksey Navalny in 2020 and was indirectly or directly responsible for his death in prison in 2024; the state also was probably behind the murder of opposition politician Boris Nemtsov in 2015. Dozens of national and regional journalists have also been killed or died in mysterious circumstances. In general, the use of repression has increased over time, and it has become at least as important as information control. After the invasion of Ukraine in 2022, the spinning and punishing both increased considerably. State television was saturated with propaganda shows about the war, and those who protested or spoke out against the war potentially could be hit with large fines or long prison sentences.

An important point about personalist autocracies is that they tend to exhibit a series of pathologies, even more so than other forms of authoritarianism. On average, they are more repressive. They are more inclined to make mistakes because they value loyalty over competence, and because sycophantic subordinates tell the leader what he or she wants to hear. They have less stable and predictable succession mechanisms and are more likely to experience violence when the ruler dies. Externally, personalist regimes are more aggressive and more inclined to make risky mistakes. Many of these features were evident in Putin's 2022 invasion of Ukraine.

Autocracy's future

In Russia's electoral authoritarianism, the noun (authoritarianism) is more important than the adjective (electoral), and the noun has become increasingly central to the Russian political regime. In a democracy, the right to rule is grounded in popular legitimacy expressed through elections. This is not how Russia's political institutions work. "The legitimacy of elections . . . is not a problem any longer for this regime," noted Russian political analyst Tatyana Stanovaya in 2021. "For Putin, his legitimacy comes from his achievements. For him, people must thank him by voting for him."

This description is the essence of personalist autocracy. Yet no ruler is forever. One way or another, Vladimir Putin will leave power at some point. What happens after a personalist autocrat leaves office depends a lot on how that happens—a coup, a revolution, a civil war, a planned resignation, death in office, and so on. Sometimes a new authoritarian ruler seamlessly takes the place of the previous one, sometimes there is an intense power struggle, sometimes the state itself is in danger of failing. And sometimes the state transitions to a more democratic government.

The formal rules of the game—that is, political institutions—do at least provide a framework for a more open and democratic government in Russia at some point in the future. Legislators could start deliberating and occasionally stand up to executive power. Courts could also restrain presidential power. Stronger regional governments could balance power in the Russian state. Political parties could compete meaningfully for power at all levels of government, and a free media could report on a range of political perspectives.

At the moment, a vision of functioning checks and balances in Russian politics is purely hypothetical. Moreover, the super-presidentialist design of the Russian Constitution makes this balance hard to achieve. Throughout the states of the former Soviet Union, those that have strong presidential power in the constitution have tended to be authoritarian, whereas those that distribute power more equally between a president, a prime minister, and the legislature have been more open politically. If Russia is to become what the constitution claims—"a democratic, federal, rule-of-law state"—it may need a new or amended constitution.

Chapter 5
Eternal state, changing society

What kind of country will the new Russia be? In the 2000s Russia returned to authoritarianism after a brief experiment with more democratic rule. To some observers, including some Russians, this was a return to Russia's natural political order, just the way things are—the need for a tsar, a "strong hand."

Most political scientists, on the other hand, are skeptical of claims that any particular country or people are destined to always live under autocracy. After all, there are only ten countries that have been continuously democratic over the past hundred years, but there are now more than a hundred democracies in the world. Most of the world's democracies were authoritarian not that long ago. If these countries can change, then Russia possibly could also.

When the Soviet Union ended and Russia became an independent country, there was considerable popular support for the notion that Russia should become a "normal country," by which people meant a wealthy democracy like in Western Europe or North America. But this support was far from universal, with many other Russians dismayed by the end of communism and the Soviet Union. As life grew harder during the 1990s, nostalgia for the old ways grew.

The Belarusian writer and Noble Prize winner Svetlana Alexievich set out to understand how Russians were thinking about what had happened and where the country was going. She described the choice as one between "great history and banal existence." One Russian framed the question this way: "Where do I want to live, in a great country or a normal one?" Some of Alexievich's interviewees claimed that "Russians need something to believe in," that "life after the fall of the empire has been boring," and that "Russia can either be great or not exist at all." Vladimir Putin's war against Ukraine appeals to those who long for imperial greatness.

Other Alexievich respondents, however, voiced their support for the normal country option. One remarked, "What do I need a great country for? I want to live in a small one like Denmark." Another response was more sarcastic: "We used to live in a great country where we stood in line for toilet paper." Alexievich shows throughout *Secondhand Time: The Last of the Soviets* that Russian society encompasses a wide range of views on Russia's past, present, and future.

The primacy of the state over society has been an enduring feature of Russian politics over the centuries. The noted nineteenth-century Russian historian Vasiliy Klyuchevskiy summed up the state-society relationship in a pithy aphorism: "The state grew fat, but the people grew lean." There is still a great deal of truth in this; the state still wields great repressive power, and society is, in many ways, weak. Some believe that this is Russia's political destiny.

In contrast, others note that Russian society today is different than it was in the past. Russians are wealthier and healthier than they have ever been. Most of them live in cities rather than rural villages, and pretty much all of them can read and write, neither of which was true a century ago. Contemporary Russians also have a lot more autonomy from the state than their Soviet-era ancestors and are connected to the outside world in ways that their predecessors could hardly imagine. For example, more than 80 percent of Russians use the Internet. Russian society is also multifaceted. Russians, like everyone else, often disagree and frequently change their minds. There is no single answer to what Russians want; rather, Russian society consists of multiple currents with uncertain futures.

Forging a new Soviet individual

In the twentieth century a new type of political system emerged in countries such as the Soviet Union and Nazi Germany—totalitarianism. Totalitarian political systems, unlike typical authoritarian systems such as military dictatorships, sought a higher degree of control over most aspects of peoples' lives in a way that went beyond depriving them of a political voice. Under totalitarianism there was supposed to be a complete politicization of society, in some sense erasing the distinction between state and society and preventing independent organizing outside the state. Political apathy was not tolerated; people were expected to demonstrate loyalty to the state. This total politicization was in pursuit of an all-encompassing ideology under the control of a mass political party, generally headed by a single dictator. The goal of total penetration of society was backed up with the use of mass terror, violence, and full control over mass media.

This type of total control could never be fully implemented in reality. Still, the Union of Soviet Socialist Republics (USSR) under Joseph Stalin from 1929 to 1953 was a prime example of this type of system. The Communist Party of the Soviet Union (CPSU) declared that the ideology of Marxism-Leninism was true and valid in all spheres of human knowledge. Stalin's cult of personality held him up as a god-like figure. Stalin and his closest associates orchestrated campaigns of state violence and terror that led to the deaths of millions.

In the decades after Stalin's death in 1953, the Soviet political system gradually shed its totalitarian aspirations, although the formal supremacy of communist ideology and the leading role of the CPSU were preserved almost until the collapse of the Soviet Union in 1991. Schoolchildren were taught about how Soviet founder Vladimir Lenin was a flawless genius, university students took required courses in Marxism-Leninism, and workers received reports on Communist Party achievements at their factories. Most people, as far as we can tell, were not actively hostile to communist rule; they were proud of the country's superpower status and space exploits (Soviet cosmonaut Yuriy Gagarin was the first man in space in 1961) and embraced the cradle-to-grave social welfare state provisions, such as "free" education, healthcare, and housing (the state obviously had to pay employees, produce building materials, and so on to make these benefits available, but the costs were not evident to average citizens).

Beneath the surface, however, the relationship between the Soviet state and society was changing in important ways. Soviet citizens found ways to develop a more private life beyond the control of the CPSU. Many people found the routines of party-promoted political life uninteresting, so they used the spaces in the existing system to engage in things they found enjoyable. In the cities, cultural offerings provided by and controlled by the state—theater, music, museums, classic literature, and so on—were readily available and cheap. Sports became an outlet for others, as well as outdoor pursuits such as hiking, camping, skiing, and amateur archaeology.

Of course, one should not romanticize the late-Soviet period. Life was often hard, and people spent a large amount of time trying to acquire things that were in short supply, including basic foodstuffs. Social pressure to conform to conventional standards, including in matters of dress and appearance, was strong. The political control of the CPSU was absolute and enforced as necessary by the KGB (Committee on State Security). Overall, though, society was changing as utopian goals faded in importance, cynicism grew about the stultifying ideology, and desires for better living standards took precedence.

The Soviet victory in the Great Patriotic War (World War II) cast a long shadow over the post-Stalin period. The enormity of the Soviet people's sacrifice and ultimate victory in the war was an important source of legitimacy for the postwar Soviet government. The war directly affected nearly every family. During the Brezhnev era (1964–1982) the victory became a more central element of Soviet ideology. Television broadcast wildly popular series about the heroic exploits of Soviet spies and soldiers during the war.

Women significantly outnumbered men after the war; in 1946 women constituted more than 60 percent of the population aged 16 and older. The shortage of adult males, combined with Soviet ideology that proclaimed the importance of women's workplace labor in building communism, meant that the USSR had one of the highest female labor-force participation rates of any country in the world. Socially, a great deal of pressure was put on Soviet women to be model workers, wives, and mothers—to produce and reproduce. The "new Soviet woman" faced a double burden, combining full-time work outside the home with responsibility for most domestic tasks. Yet sexist social norms also meant that in the workplace and in political life most leadership positions were held by men. In the classic Oscar-winning 1980 Soviet film, *Moscow Does Not Believe in Tears*, the heroine has a successful career and atypically had risen to the position of factory director, but she is depicted as unfulfilled and in need of a man to bring her happiness.

When Mikhail Gorbachev came to power in 1985, there was little reason to think that the relationship between the Soviet state and the people was broken. The leader of one of Russia's most famous rock bands, Time Machine (*Mashina Vremeni*), reflected in 1994, "It had never even occurred to me that in the Soviet Union anything could ever change. Let alone that it could disappear. No one expected it. Neither children, nor adults. There was a complete impression that everything was forever."

Gorbachev's policy of *glasnost* (openness), originally intended to uncover bureaucratic opponents of his attempt to reform the system and overcome the stagnation of the Brezhnev era, quickly turned into a revolutionary reexamination of the entire Soviet past. In the late 1980s even Soviet founder Vladimir Lenin came under criticism. Prior to that he was an officially revered figure. In January 1991 a young Russian actor and musician appeared on Soviet TV in an absurdist mock-interview in which he impersonated a historian who had discovered that Lenin was in fact a mushroom. By the end of the year the Soviet Union was gone.

Transitional citizens

The Soviet Union ceased to exist, and a new Russian Federation— and 14 other countries—arose from its ashes. Yet the people were still the same. They were, in the words of Harvard political scientist Timothy Colton, "transitional citizens." Most of the political leaders, including the new president, Boris Yeltsin, had been card-carrying members of the CPSU. Indeed, the Soviet political and economic order was the only one that almost anyone still alive could remember. Could the typical Soviet man and woman quickly adjust to the new way of life?

There were some causes for optimism. The last years of the USSR had been a heady time in which people experienced more freedom than they had in their lives. Long-forbidden texts were published in a great rush in the late 1980s and early 1990s. For the first time since 1917, meaningful elections with uncertain results were held starting in 1989. Society started to organize itself in new informal organizations not controlled by the CPSU. Protestors took to the streets, first in small numbers but ultimately by the hundreds of thousands. One participant, looking back on the dramatic events of 1991, reminisced, "We were triumphant, we were powerful. We wanted to live. We were intoxicated by freedom." In a poll taken in 1992, Russians said that the most positive value was freedom and the least positive one was Marxism-Leninism.

At the same time, for many people the revolutionary changes brought about by the death of the Soviet Union were disorienting. The rights and responsibilities of democratic citizenship were unfamiliar. The rapid economic shift from state planning to market capitalism led to hyperinflation and economic dislocation. People were drunk on freedom, but they also had to eat. The violent constitutional showdown in October 1993 followed a year later by the bloody Chechen War were further sources of disillusionment.

Since the 1990s, public opinion polls in Russia have shown a profound level of distrust in most state institutions. In the 1990s no state institution had the full confidence of more than 40 percent of Russians, and some of them—such as the parliament and political parties—had the full confidence of fewer than 10 percent. The most popular state institution was the army, gaining the full support of 30 to 40 percent of Russians in the 1990s, but only a small minority (20–25 percent) of Russians wanted a close relative to serve in the military. Comparing these results with other countries, one sociologist declared that trust in state bodies in Russia was the lowest in the world.

The term "civil society" refers to that sphere of activity that exists outside the family yet beyond the control of the state and includes everything from religious organizations, to sports leagues, to community organizations, to politically oriented nongovernmental organizations (NGOs). A true civil society can cooperate with the state, but it cannot be controlled by the state. Civil society after communism's demise did emerge, but it was weak. After the dramatic burst of social and political activity in the late 1980s and early 1990s, there was a retreat into private life. Russians relied on the strong friendship networks they had built under communism to get through a difficult period. There was no tradition of private charitable giving or corporate philanthropy after 70 years of Soviet rule. The Russian state had little money to financially support a nascent civil society, although in the 1990s it did create a legal structure for independent civil society organizations. Despite many obstacles, some NGOs developed national reputations, such as the Committee of Soldiers' Mothers of Russia, which defended the rights of military draftees and enlisted personnel.

For better or worse, much of the slack in financial support was taken up by foreign funders, whether governments or foreign foundations. On the positive side, foreign funding helped nurture a young and emergent civil society. On the negative side, NGOs dependent on outside money sometimes became disconnected from their own domestic constituents and tailored their activities more to foreign priorities. Russian civil society was coming alive, and there was quite a bit of variation across the massive country, but its grassroots in local communities were still weak.

Living through communism affected not only civil society development but also public attitudes. Compared with citizens in countries that did not experience communism, Russians were more inclined to support state provision of social welfare and were less supportive of democracy and free markets. Russians were not unique in this respect; similar results were observable in post-communist countries in Eastern Europe and the rest of the former Soviet Union. These effects were stronger in those countries that had spent a longer period of time under communism, such as Russia.

If Russian society was weak and in transition, so too was the Russian state, which was trying to maintain political order and enforce its rules at a time when it had new borders that were themselves in dispute. Its own officials were not trained or prepared to operate under new conditions. The American historian Stephen Kotkin asked pointedly, "How was the incoherent Russian state going to solve the country's problems when the state *was* the main problem?"

The 1990s, then, was a time of enormous change for both Russian society and the Russian state. The lofty hopes of quickly becoming a "normal country" with an efficient and responsive state and a robust and well-organized civil society were dashed. Russia had suffered through a difficult decade, but it did have a new constitutional system that provided some regularity, and a new economy was taking shape. Russian society had shown its resilience in important ways, even if its capacity for self-organization was only starting to develop. Starting in 1999 the economy began to grow rapidly. Would the new millennium lead to a fundamental transformation in the traditional state-society relationship, bringing forth a new one built on cooperation and mutual support?

Putin's people

Vladimir Putin made his view of the proper state-society relationship clear at the very end of 1999, one day before he took over the presidency from Boris Yeltsin. In a lengthy article laying out his vision for Russia, he prioritized rebuilding the primacy of the Russian state:

> "A strong state for a Russian is not an anomaly, not something to fight against, but on the contrary is the source and guarantor of order, the initiator and driving force of any change. . . . Russia needs strong state power and must have it."

A few months later, in early 2000, he further drove the point home: "Russia from the very beginning was created as a super-centralized state. It is fixed in her genetic code, her traditions, the mentality of the people."

Putin's views about the primacy of the state played an important role in the authoritarian turn he pursued as ruler. Conceptually, there is no reason to equate a strong state with an authoritarian one—indeed, many of the world's most effective and competent states are also its most democratic—but in Putin's interpretation the only way to restore order and stability was by creating a "super-centralized state" that weakened other sources of power. He believed that society's role was to come together, support the authorities, embrace patriotism, and thereby help Russia return to greatness.

Putin was instantly popular. His public approval rating was over 60 percent when he took power and has remained there basically ever since. When asked about which politicians they trust, rather than being asked specifically about approval for Putin, Russians express less support for Putin, with "trust" figures lagging 20 to 30 points behind "approval" numbers. Even then, however, Putin remains by far the most trusted politician in the country.

Why do Russians support Putin? The reasons have changed over time. In the 2000s, what we might call "early Putinism," he received high marks for raising living standards, raising hope and optimism, and developing the economy. Since the annexation of Crimea in 2014, a period we might call "high Putinism," Putin's popularity has primarily been associated with foreign policy and security issues, such as rebuilding the military and raising Russia's international standing. As economic stagnation set in after 2013, his former strength in domestic matters, such as raising living standards, has become an area of relative weakness. Throughout his rule, Putin has received his lowest rating on the issue of corruption and his failure to combat it.

Putin's popularity raises an important question: If Russians support Putin, and Putin is a dictator, then do Russians support dictatorship? In a word, no. Social scientists have learned quite a lot over the past several decades about what Russians think about democracy. Like citizens in many countries, especially formerly authoritarian ones, Russians often have trouble defining democracy clearly. They are just as inclined to list a high standard of living as free and fair elections when asked to define democracy. However, despite some confusion about what exactly democracy is, Russians tend to support its features when asked about them separately, such as fair elections, competition between political parties, and basic democratic rights such as freedom of speech.

On the other hand, this support for the elements of democracy is not overwhelming. In general, Russians cannot seem to decide for themselves or agree among each other about how democratic Russia is or how democratic it should become. There is not a lot of clamoring for more authoritarianism, but neither is there a strong contingent pushing for more democracy.

In important ways, more than three decades after the Soviet collapse, Putin's people are still transitional citizens. This transition experience has strongly shaped societal views. The period of the most freedom and highest levels of democracy, from the late 1980s to the mid-1990s, is also associated in the popular mind with chaos and economic depression. In contrast, during Putin's first two terms as president, real wages tripled. One can argue about how much the depression of the 1990s was Yeltsin's fault and how much the boom of the 2000s was Putin's achievement, but for most Russians the 1990s are associated with instability and hardship and the decade after with more stability and greater well-being. Given this association, for some Russians the very word "democracy" (*demokratiya*) is a dirty word; indeed, the Russian word for democracy, with the change or addition of one letter, can be transformed into made-up words meaning either "stealing from the people" (*demokradiya*) or "shitocracy" (*dermokratiya*).

By the 2000s, many Russians were tired of politics. This popular exhaustion with politics fit comfortably with Putin's ideas about rebuilding strong state power. Russians were more willing to accept a strongman leader like Putin who promised to combine democracy and order. In the 2000s, as the Russian journalist Maria Lipman observed, there was a "non-intrusion pact" in which the people would stay out of politics and the state would stay out of the people's lives. As one Russian put it, "Our job is to go and vote for the right candidate then call it a day."

The state-society relationship under Putin was not, however, built only upon negative images of the 1990s. Over time, a more positive set of beliefs was necessary. For Putin, this positive agenda was built on a foundation of patriotism and notions of Russian distinctiveness and greatness. The Great Patriotic War was at the centerpiece of this agenda. The war was the one historical event upon which almost all Russians could agree. Under Putin, the May 9 Victory Day Parade became one of the key events on Russia's political calendar. "The day became less about remembering the war dead," observed British journalist Shaun Walker, "and more about projecting the military might of contemporary Russia." The celebration of the Soviet war victory meshed well with leadership beliefs that emphasized Russia's status as an exceptional country that is able to withstand hardships and overcome hostile enemies that want to destroy it.

State control over television helped build societal support for its patriotic message, which connected a great Russia with the need to have Putin as the country's great leader. All of the major Russian television channels are in the hands of the Russian state or Putin's close personal associates. These channels are much more sophisticated, slick, and technologically advanced than their Soviet predecessors, and they are the most important source of news for many Russians. TV channels push a narrative of Russia "rising from its knees" after enduring humiliation by the West following the Soviet breakdown. This narrative resonates strongly and emotionally with many Russians.

8. A bare-chested Vladimir Putin rides a horse while on vacation in Siberia, August 2009. Putin's image, especially in the first decade of his rule, was based around presenting him as a strong masculine leader.

Controlling society

In addition to positive narratives about a strong state and great Russia, state repression has been an important tool for managing society. For a typical citizen with only a passing interest in politics, Russia was generally freer than in the Soviet past. At least before the 2022 full-scale invasion of Ukraine, there was little censorship in such areas as movies, books, and theater. Until around 2020, the Internet had been mostly uncensored and free-wheeling, and until the 2022 war, Russians had access to Western social media sites such as Facebook and Twitter, a sharp difference from a more repressive authoritarian country like China. Unlike during the Soviet period, the borders are open, so most Russians can travel outside the country, although only about 30 percent of them have foreign travel passports. For the first two decades of the Putin era, life remained much freer than in the Soviet Union in most respects.

On the other hand, in the twenty-first century the state has gradually ratcheted up repression of societal actors involved in oppositional politics or even civil society work in certain spheres, such as human rights or environmental politics. Most Russian NGOs work in the social sphere, including issues such as welfare services, education, charity, and so on. Government support for such nonpolitical NGOs increased. In contrast, NGOs working on political issues faced increasing political pressure. In essence, the Russian state distinguishes between "good NGOs" that help the state and can subsist on state funding and "bad NGOs" that are seen as threats to the state and thus subject to restrictions and bans. This approach reflects a view of the state-society relationship that elevates state interests over societal ones and limits the ability of societal actors to monitor the state and hold it accountable to society—a key task of civil society in democratic countries.

In principle, elections are another means of holding the state accountable. Under Russia's electoral authoritarian system, elections are not fair. In December 2011, however, popular anger over falsified Duma election results led to large popular protests for several months, especially in Moscow. The biggest demonstrations that winter were estimated to have between 60,000 and 100,000 participants, making them the largest rallies in Moscow since the Soviet collapse. The state became more repressive after this brief protest wave. Fines for participating in protests increased dramatically, and protestors also faced the prospect of arrest and prison sentences. The tacit "non-intrusion pact" from the 2000s was being replaced with a new political line that distinguished between loyal and patriotic Russians and those who subscribed to alien, foreign-inspired beliefs and sought to undermine Russia's conservative political order.

No episode better illustrates the Kremlin's new approach to state-society relations than the Pussy Riot affair. Pussy Riot is a feminist punk performance art collective founded in 2011. In February 2012 several members of the group, wearing their signature colorful dresses, tights, and balaclavas, briefly danced and jumped around in front of the altar of the Cathedral of Christ the Savior in central Moscow before church security intervened. Pussy Riot released video footage of this "punk prayer" entitled "Mother of God, Drive Putin Away." The song's profane lyrics call on the Virgin Mary to get rid of Putin and become a feminist. The song also critiques the close links between the Russian Orthodox Church and the state, calling the church's patriarch a "bitch" and saying he should believe in God rather than Putin.

When three members of Pussy Riot were arrested for "hooliganism . . . motivated by religious hatred or hostility," their case became an international cause célèbre. American journalist Joshua Yaffa observed, "For Putin, Pussy Riot was a godsend: an opportunity to paint those opposed to his rule as a bunch of godless freaks and punks who made a mockery of Russia's most sacred traditions." The judge in the case called attention to Pussy Riot's feminist beliefs as evidence of the "religious hatred" that motivated their actions. The three women were sentenced to two years in prison, although one of them later got the sentence reduced to probation. The Pussy Riot case was symbolic of the close relationship between the Russian Orthodox Church and state authorities in contemporary Russia, and an indication of the government's embrace of a conservative social message that contrasted Russia's spiritual traditions with the purported liberal decadence of the West.

From that point forward, Putin embraced the message that Russia has a duty to promote "traditional values." Putin depicted these values as under threat from a decadent West. The state criminalized "gay propaganda" and derided LGBT rights and feminism. In 2022 Putin accused Western elites of promoting "perversions that lead to degradation and extinction" and

9. Pussy Riot protests against Russian ruler Vladimir Putin on Red Square in January 2012. Two of its members served two years in prison for their protest at a Moscow cathedral in February 2012.

"Satanism." The following year, Russian senator Margarita Pavlova stated that rather than directing young women toward higher education, the state should encourage them to have more children. The state and the Russian Orthodox Church promoted the notion that traditional values in Russia were under threat from liberal Western elites.

A more punitive approach toward those social actors who challenged the state became evident in politics as well. The life and political career of opposition leader Aleksey Navalny demonstrates well this policy of tightening the screws. Navalny entered into politics in the 2000s, while still a young man in his mid-20s. He eventually rose to prominence as a blogger, anticorruption crusader, and one of the organizers of the 2011–2012 protests. He demonstrated a talent for public politics, including a gift for pithy, colorful slogans—he labeled United Russia the "party of swindlers and thieves"—and adept use of social media (blogs, YouTube, Twitter, Instagram, and so on).

To many people's surprise, Navalny was allowed to run for mayor of Moscow in 2013. Although he was denied access to state television, he ran an effective grassroots campaign with a young and motivated group of volunteers. He finished a solid second place with 27 percent of the vote; the incumbent, Putin ally Sergey Sobyanin, won with 51 percent. After that performance, Navalny was never again allowed on the ballot for any office. Nevertheless, he continued to be a thorn in the side of the authorities because of his popular YouTube videos investigating corruption by top government officials and his grassroots organizing around the country.

Navalny was the victim of an attempted assassination in August 2020; he was poisoned with a banned chemical agent known as Novichok. In a remarkable twist, while recuperating in Germany, Navalny was able to use his investigative skills—and those of a group of investigative journalists—to provide overwhelming evidence that he had been trailed for years by a team of FSB (Federal Security Service) agents; Navalny even managed to trick one of these agents into discussing the details of the assassination effort in a direct call to the agent's cell phone. Experts believe that such an FSB operation would have required approval from President Putin.

Navalny made a dramatic return to Moscow from Germany in January 2021 and was immediately arrested. Two days after his return, his Anti-Corruption Foundation released its biggest investigative film ever (watched more than 100 million times), *Putin's Palace: History of the World's Largest Bribe*. The film focuses primarily on a massive palace on the Black Sea shore that, according to the investigation, was built specifically for Putin and was estimated to cost over one billion dollars. Navalny's arrest triggered some of the largest protests Russia had seen in years, even though it was the depth of winter and the protests were declared illegal. Protestors came out in nearly 200 cities and towns around the country. The arrest and imprisonment of Navalny precipitated a broader crackdown on opposition political forces, his organizations were closed down, and his key associates were forced to flee the country. Navalny died in prison in February 2024 at the age of 47; regardless of exactly what happened on the day Navalny died, Putin and the Russian state were responsible for his death, having poisoned him and then locked him away in extremely harsh prison conditions, much of which he spent in solitary confinement.

The future of Russian state primacy

The Russian state crackdown on social opposition, such as activists and independent journalists, accelerated sharply after the 2022 invasion of Ukraine. The state closed down all independent media still working inside the country, repressed antiwar protests, and enacted new criminal penalties for opposing the war (or even calling it a war rather than a "special military operation"). Police detained protesters for standing alone on a street holding a piece of paper with slogans such as "thou shalt not kill," "no war," "two words" (assumed to mean "no war"); people holding blank pieces of paper were also detained. A pacifist and feminist activist from Saint Petersburg was sentenced to seven years in jail for replacing price tags in a supermarket with antiwar slogans.

Public opinion polls showed a majority of Russians supported the war, although experts disagreed on whether polls under repressive wartime conditions provided accurate information. People under 40 and those from major cities generally were less positive about the war. A generation gap in Russian surveys became noticeable in the late 2010s. Compared with older generations, young Russians are more inclined to get their news from the Internet than from television, and are more pro-business, more positive about human rights, more tolerant of gays and minorities, and more pro-Western. Social attitudes about household matters such as housework and childrearing are changing toward greater gender equality. Putin's approval rating fell sharply among Russian youth (ages 18–24) after 2018, opening up a more than 20 percent gap between the young and those over 55.

The prospect of generational change leading to political change, however, is highly uncertain. As time goes on, fewer and fewer people will have memories of the Soviet period, the disintegration of the USSR, and the difficult transition years of the 1990s. Over time, it is possible that a new attitude toward the state will arise. Older Russians have been conditioned to have high expectations of the state in terms of what it promises, but also a sense of realism or even resignation about how much it will actually deliver. As the political scientist Samuel Greene observed in 2017, Russians tend to see the state "as simultaneously dysfunctional and yet legitimate, unjust and yet worthy." Engagement with the state is necessary to get things that people want and need, but people also try to live their lives *around* the state, avoiding it rather than confronting it when necessary.

The state, however, is unavoidable. Many Russians are dependent on the state, either because they are retirees receiving pensions or because they work for the state or state-owned enterprises. The primacy of the state over society has been a relatively constant feature of Russian life for centuries. The end of the communist experiment in 1991 meant a retrenchment in the overwhelmingly dominant role of the state in political, economic, and social life. For many, the retreat of the state in the 1990s went too far, leaving people to fend for themselves, although some welcomed the greater freedom and autonomy of that decade.

Putin's efforts to reassert the primacy of the state have in many respects been a success—the state is definitely on top and possesses many tools to shape its image and impose its will. Yet its ability to carry out some of its core tasks—building and maintaining roads, upholding public order, delivering healthcare and other services—frequently falls short of popular expectations. Russians are much more inclined to think that Putin represents the interests of big business and state employees, especially those from the military and security services, than the interests of the middle and working classes.

Russians are not the only people in the world who are often cynical about politics and politicians and try to avoid spending too much time interacting with the political world, but it seems to be a particularly pronounced phenomenon in Russia. "Indifference has always provided the social foundation of the Putin regime: a state indifferent to its citizens and separate from them, a society indifferent to the state and separate from it," observed Russian analyst Andrei Kolesnikov. Under such circumstances, politics is often dominated by so-called elites—a small subset of society that is particularly involved in and influential in politics. Russian politics depends a great deal on these elites—the president and those who can influence him.

Chapter 6
Tsars and courtiers

The most basic political stories start with leaders. American schoolchildren impress adults by reciting the names of every American president in order, a chronology most adults have long since forgotten. Shakespeare's history plays all bear the name of an English king, who is the center of the action. In Russia, one of the most popular *matryoshka* (nesting) dolls for tourists is a historical series of leaders, culminating with a Vladimir Putin doll.

Leaders and elites matter everywhere—by definition, they are those charged with primary responsibility for governing a country, or who are particularly influential in politics. They especially matter in authoritarian political systems, which are marked either by oligarchy (rule of the few) or autocracy (rule of one), as opposed to democracies (rule of the people).

Russia has almost always been authoritarian. There is no longer a formal royal court, as there was in the tsarist era, nor is there a titled nobility. Yet access to and influence with the leader, often referred to informally as "the tsar" or "the boss," still greatly shapes Russian politics.

In the Russian Empire's first and only official census (1897), Tsar Nicholas II listed his occupation as "master of the Russian land." His actual title was not merely Tsar but "Emperor and Autocrat of

All the Russias." Nicholas II believed firmly in the principle of autocracy and his divinely ordained responsibility for ruling Russia—power that he was forced to surrender during the 1917 revolution.

For Nicholas and his predecessors, autocratic rule was the natural political system for Russia. Only God and their conscience limited their power. Tsars were not answerable to or seriously constrained by the landed nobility, the church, or any legal authority, and certainly not by their subjects. Compared with monarchs in Western Europe, whose relations with society developed from a feudal order of mutual obligation between kings and lords, Russian tsars presided over a very centralized political system in which their claim to power and ownership of the state and its territory was relatively unchecked.

A political system built entirely upon the will of one person sounds, to be frank, implausible. The emperor or empress, after all, was just one person. Historians of Russia have long debated how literally we should take the claims of unconstrained Russian autocracy. In reality, of course, there were some limits on the ruler's power. There were traditions and customs that had some force, and the military-landowning class also possessed great power, and on occasion could curb the tsar's supremacy or even overthrow him. Courtiers conducted several palace coups in the eighteenth century, and Catherine II's son Paul I was assassinated in his own bedroom by a group of disgruntled noble officers. In general, though, Russian tsars were extremely powerful and faced fewer constraints from elites than most other European rulers.

Soviet leaders were also rulers with a great deal of power. Joseph Stalin was the most dominant and unconstrained Soviet dictator, turning the repressive apparatus of the Soviet state against other top Communist Party officials in the bloody "Great Purge" between 1936 and 1938. He even had the wives of several top officials sent to the Gulag. Given the totalitarian nature of Stalin's regime, with no independent economic or social actors and a cult of the leader, Stalin's power was colossal. Of course, other top officials wielded power in their own realms and competed to curry favor with Stalin, but all the top decisions belonged to him.

After Stalin's death in 1953, the new watchword was "collective leadership." Greater emphasis was placed on the power of the Communist Party as an institution. Over time, Stalin's successors as General Secretary tended to acquire considerable individual power, yet the system never returned to personalist dictatorship. The system became an oligarchy, not an autocracy. Even so, the degree to which a tactically skillful leader like Mikhail Gorbachev could totally upend the political order demonstrates that the tradition of a dominant leader endured in the Soviet Union.

The pattern of strong chief executives continued in post-Soviet Russia. The super-presidential 1993 constitution made it difficult for the legislature to constrain the president, although in the 1990s under Boris Yeltsin the opposition's parliamentary majority meant it could sometimes thwart his wishes. By the end of Vladimir Putin's first term as president in 2004, however, he had engineered a subservient legislature. Russia was moving toward a personalist dictatorship that looked less and less like the rule of the few and more and more like the rule of one man.

Putinism is not really the rule of one man. Various elites have much more influence than average Russians, either because they are wealthy and control important businesses or because they occupy a state position that allows them to have some influence in their sphere. Most of the top elites are longtime associates of Putin who hold these positions because of their connections to him. At the regional level, there are also political and economic elites with disproportionate sway, within the overall parameters set by the Kremlin.

Still, the system looks more like the relationship between a tsar and his courtiers than a real sharing of power. In 2023 the

Russian political analyst Tatyana Stanovaya poured cold water on the notion that, given the disastrous invasion of Ukraine, the elite would rise up and replace Putin. "We do not have an elite that one could consider a political force, which has a plan, ambitions, an agenda—there is no such force," Stanovaya said. "There is only Putin and an apparatus serving him."

Perhaps the most important thing to understand about this elite, such as it is, is that "informal" relationships and connections matter more than the formal position that someone holds in the political system. The term "informal" is meant to draw a distinction between the formal legal rules of the game, such as those contained in the constitution, and unwritten rules and understandings that are not legally codified but are widely shared.

Informal norms and personal connections matter everywhere. Yet the extent to which they matter varies over time and place. They tend to matter less in democratic countries with strong laws and formal institutions in which ideologically different political parties compete at regular intervals, with power frequently changing hands. Conversely, informal rules and connections tend to matter more in a country like Russia where the legal system is weak.

Social scientists have used a variety of terms to refer to political systems in which politics is more about battles behind the scenes between informal groupings of elites than the formal rules and laws. The political scientist Henry Hale, in an influential book on politics in Eastern Europe and Eurasia, calls these types of systems "patronal." In patronal political systems, people seek political and economic gain largely through personal connections to friends and acquaintances. These acquaintances have their own groups of friends and acquaintances, and these webs of connections between people are networks that members can use to help each other and get ahead. The most powerful people at the top of these informal networks are called "patrons" (the Latin root of the word comes from "father" and can also mean defender, protector, lord, or master). Weaker people in these networks are called "clients." People in intermediate positions are both patrons and clients. According to Hale, to understand politics in countries like Russia, we should think less about ideas and laws and think more about connections, favors, and mutual loyalty. Importantly, patronal political systems are not some kind of deviation from the norm, but rather the main way politics has been organized in most societies throughout history.

These types of patronal relationships have existed in Russia throughout its history. When newly independent Russia adopted a constitution in 1993, some hoped that Russia could move away from this patronal past and create a democratic, rule-of-law state in which free competition between political parties determined who governed. There were some signs that this was taking place, both at the national level and in some Russian regions. But observers quickly noticed that some people had a lot of influence that was not connected to their formal position in the state, and that parallel to the battle between different political parties there was an arguably more important set of battles between different informal groupings. Analysts have dubbed these groupings "clans," which just means a close-knit group of powerful individuals who work together to increase their power and wealth.

As early as 1995, an American diplomat in Moscow argued in a Russian newspaper that people watching the public competition between the executive and legislative branches, or between different political parties, were missing the real action. The real action, he said, was the fight between different political-economic clans, all connected loosely to Russian President Boris Yeltsin but working to pursue the narrow interests of their group. Some of the patrons heading these clans were also constitutionally powerful, like the prime minister, whereas others had influence far beyond their formal position, like Yeltsin's bodyguard.

When Vladimir Putin took over as president in 2000, a similar pattern occurred. Putin placed his close acquaintances and allies in positions of power in Russian politics and business, and they used their connections to advance their power and interests. Groups connected to Yeltsin eventually lost their influence or were incorporated into Putin's system. By the end of his first two terms as president in early 2008, nearly every top official was connected to Putin personally either through a shared KGB (Committee on State Security) background, where Putin worked from 1975 until 1991, or because they worked together in Saint Petersburg in the early 1990s, when Putin was deputy mayor. This included the prime minister; the defense minister; the finance minister; the heads of the key security services; the speaker and chairman of the two houses of parliament (the Duma and the Federation Council); the heads of the biggest state-owned gas, oil, and pipeline companies; the head of Russian Railroads (the biggest employer in Russia); the head of the main state weapons-manufacturing company; and on and on.

Despite this dominance of Putin's associates, Putin did not have one unified team. For example, there were rivalries between those with backgrounds in law and economics versus those with backgrounds in the KGB and other security services. The divisions were not always clear-cut. For example, it was sometimes assumed that everyone who came from the KGB was part of one team or clan with shared views and interests, but in reality common backgrounds did not always lead to membership in the same "clan." So-called Kremlinologists—people who study Russian elite politics—could not always agree on who was affiliated with this or that clan. But they all agreed that to really understand Russian politics, you needed to look beneath the surface and trace the informal connections and identify the most powerful "patrons."

Hale observed that in patronal societies there is still a role for the formal political institutions. In particular, in a country like Russia with a "super-presidential" constitution the president tends to be the most important patron in the system, with the different clans connected to him (the last female ruler in Russia was Catherine II, more than two centuries ago) and battling for his favor. Hale calls this a "single pyramid" system, with the most powerful groups focused on pleasing the boss at the top and dependent on him. But in a different constitutional system, in which power is distributed more evenly— such as between a president and a prime minister, or with a more powerful parliament—then there might be multiple competing pyramids, which helps preserve a more open political system.

Yeltsin was never powerful enough to bring all the competing clans under his control, so during the 1990s Russia did not really operate like a true single pyramid system. But Putin, as a younger and more popular leader with a stronger desire to bring everything under his control, was able to build a true single pyramid. At first, Putin shifted Russia's political system from a semi-democratic one to an authoritarian one. Over time, he also moved Russia along the authoritarian continuum from a more competitive oligarchy to something closer to an autocratic system like that seen under the tsars or Stalin.

10. **President Vladimir Putin meets with the Russian Security Council on the eve of the full-scale invasion of Ukraine in February 2022. The seating arrangement reflected both Putin's fears about COVID-19 and his dominant position in Russian politics.**

Putin's dominance over the rest of the top elite was plainly evident in a prominent meeting of the Security Council, which includes most of Russia's most powerful officials, on the eve of the full-scale invasion of Ukraine in February 2022. Rather than sitting around a table together, Putin sat alone at a desk in the ornate Catherine's Hall in the Kremlin, with the other officials seated far away on separate chairs arranged in a semicircle. One by one, these officials were called upon to endorse Putin's plans for Ukraine. Most strikingly, Putin badgered one of his closest allies, Sergey Naryshkin, repeatedly interrupting him and admonishing him to "speak plainly." When Naryshkin got his lines wrong (he endorsed the wrong proposal) and was corrected by Putin, he looked like he wanted to sink into the floor. Naryshkin was not some nobody. He was, like Putin, a former KGB officer from Leningrad who had held such top positions as chairman of the Duma, Kremlin chief of staff, and head of the Foreign Intelligence Service. The meeting, large fragments of which were broadcast on state television, was a stark demonstration of Putin's tsar-like status in Russia's personalistic autocracy.

The pursuit of power and wealth

What do rulers and elites want? Many political scientists assume that politicians are narrowly self-interested and rational and pursue personal goals, especially getting and retaining power. Even if politicians might have other goals, such as enacting policy changes, they can only do so if they have power. Elites might also pursue other forms of personal gain, such as wealth. Power and wealth, of course, can often go together, with money giving someone more power, and power making it easier to acquire money. Other experts disagree with this assumption, contending that elites also care about ideas and policies. But given the considerable evidence that Russia is very corrupt, it makes sense to begin by "following the money." In a corrupt political system, state officials use their position to enrich themselves. In its most

extreme form, the political system is described as a kleptocracy—
"the rule of thieves."

Putin's Russia has indeed often been described as a kleptocracy,
both by foreign experts and opposition Russian politicians like
Aleksey Navalny, who built his political career attacking official
corruption. It is impossible to prove exactly how wealthy Vladimir
Putin is. But anticorruption activists, especially Navalny's team,
and investigative journalists have proved rather conclusively that
Putin and his family are lavishly wealthy. These investigations
have uncovered mansions in Russia, additional property in
prestigious cities in Europe, yachts, expensive watches and
clothes, and so on.

Many other close Putin associates, other top officials, and their
relatives are also extremely wealthy, far beyond their income as
state officials. The most famous cases inspired Internet memes,
like the duck house at former President Dmitriy Medvedev's secret
country estate, or the special repository for fur coats allegedly
built in the palace of the former head of the state company
Russian Railroads, Vladimir Yakunin. Both Medvedev and
Yakunin were, like Putin, born in Leningrad; Yakunin served in
the Soviet KGB, and Medvedev worked in the Saint Petersburg
mayor's office in the early 1990s. Putin has surrounded himself
with loyalists.

Russia ranks very highly on worldwide indexes of corruption. For
example, the World Bank's Worldwide Governance Indicators for
"control of corruption" in 2021 ranked Russia in the 20th
percentile for corruption, meaning 80 percent of the countries in
the world are less corrupt than Russia. Although Russia is a
relatively wealthy country, in terms of corruption it is on the level
of the world's poorest countries. The international NGO
Transparency International in 2021 ranked Russia 137th out of
180 countries in the world in its Corruption Perceptions Index,

tied with Mali and Paraguay. For comparison's sake, the United States ranked 24th and China ranked 65th.

The problem is not that Russians are inherently crooked or dishonest. In an experiment conducted in countries around the world, Russians were roughly as likely as Americans or the British to return a "lost" wallet with cash inside. Rather, the widespread nature of corruption is better explained by a combination of historical factors, such as generally weak property rights and a traditional reliance on informal networks, and political ones, such as a personalist autocracy with weak institutions and a weak rule of law.

The Russian political scientist Kirill Rogov described Russia as a country with "soft legal constraints." It is not that rules and laws do not exist—there are many of them in Russia—and not even that they are badly enforced. Rather, there are "informal rules about the violation of the formal rules." The state has the power to grant—or not grant—the right to ignore the law. This "on/off switch" gives a big advantage to those whose violation of the law is ignored, and especially to those who decide who gets to break the rules.

The security services and law enforcement organs collect compromising information, referred to as *kompromat* in Russian, and use it to control and blackmail the elite. A vivid example of this process and how these "soft legal constraints" work came to light in 2018 when Alexander Shestun, the head of an administrative district in the greater Moscow region, released secretly recorded conversations between him and an FSB general. The general had visited Shestun and pressured him to resign his post because of a conflict with the region's governor. The FSB general told Shestun that if he did not resign, "they will attack you from all sides: criminal investigators, prosecutors, you'll be surrounded. . . . They'll take you away, they'll seize your assets. . . . They'll flatten you. . . . You'll go to jail." And Shestun did indeed go to jail, sentenced to 15 years in a high-security prison for fraud, money laundering, and bribery.

Shestun may or may not have been guilty of these crimes. The political issue is that the Russian state uses evidence of corruption as a means of control over the elites. The FSB general talking to Shestun bragged, "I work on all governors, all mayors, on all regions." Law enforcement agencies play a crucial role in the system of "soft legal constraints" because they control the on/off switch.

This power of law enforcement agencies makes them some of the most corrupt state agencies. Their very impunity is a temptation. Evidence of their corruption comes out during periodic struggles for control between competing law enforcement agencies, which fight for the right to control both legal and illegal forms of economic activity. For example, in 2016 a Russian police colonel was arrested with the equivalent of more than $100 million in his apartment; at the time he headed a unit responsible for fighting corruption. At the same time, law enforcement agencies have little power to go after politically connected elites and their corruption. The informal rules of elite politics in Russia follow the Latin American saying, "For my friends, everything; for my enemies, the law." The Russian state is both supreme and unconstrained, presenting many opportunities for the tsar and his courtiers to enrich themselves.

The will of the tsar

Putin once described himself as "working like a galley slave" as president. The former political opposition leader Boris Nemtsov, who was assassinated near the Kremlin in 2015, published an exposé detailing Putin's luxurious lifestyle under the mocking title, "The Life of a Galley Slave." Yet Putin was probably quite sincere in thinking that he worked very hard for Russia, and that he deserved to live at least as well as the wealthy oligarchs who, in his view, were not nearly as patriotic and indispensable to the Russian state as he was. Putin and other top officials likely see no contradiction between enriching themselves and working to advance Russia's interests as they see them.

The Russian Constitution grants the president the power to "determine the main directions of domestic and foreign policy." Besides his considerable formal powers, Putin, as the "boss" at the top of a single-pyramid system, has a lot of informal authority as well. In olden times, "the will of the tsar" was sufficient to define Russian state policy, and to an important extent that is true today.

However, it is not always easy to know what Putin wants. In general, you can infer what someone wants based on what they say and what they do, and the same basic approach can be applied to Putin. But it is complicated. He talks a lot, but sometimes he lies or dissembles. He does things, but the intent of this or that policy is not always clear. Still, given that Putin has been the dominant leader of Russia for the majority of its time as an independent state, understanding what Putin and his close associates think is an important part of understanding Russia politics.

There have been many attempts to analyze Putin. Fiona Hill and Clifford Gaddy, longtime Russia watchers, wrote an analytical biography that tried to tackle the "who is Mr. Putin?" question. They weave together multiple influences on his worldview: the perceived need to restore order and build a strong state that dominates society, his obsession with his conception of Russia's history, the deep-seated feeling that Russia must struggle to survive in a hostile world, the necessity of using the power of the state to control business and keep it in line, and his own status as an outsider with a chip on his shoulder—a self-described childhood "hooligan" who found discipline with the martial arts as a teenager. Although observers have sometimes portrayed Putin as a bloodless bureaucrat, especially early in his career, it is clear he has strong views and feelings that shape what he does.

Putin's way of thinking reflects three key themes. First, he repeatedly stresses the importance of a Russian state that is strong both at home and abroad, which he considers crucial to maintaining Russia's great power status. Second, and with equal frequency, he talks about the revolutionary crisis Russia experienced after the Soviet collapse and gives himself credit for ending it and restoring order. Finally, the relationship between Russia and the West is a constant theme in his speeches; for most of his presidency, Putin has complained that Russia is treated unfairly by a West that seeks to weaken or even destroy it.

These themes all came together during a triumphal September 2022 speech in the Kremlin's Saint George's Hall to mark the illegal annexation of four regions of Ukraine during the Russo-Ukraine War. Putin spent most of his speech denouncing the West for its ongoing perfidy toward Russia. He maintained that the West wanted Russia to "fall to pieces" during "the horrible 1990s, hungry, cold, and hopeless." Putin argued Russia's success against Western efforts to subdue it was because of his creation of "a strong centralized state."

Putin's hostility toward the West is not shared by all Russians, nor by all elites. Moreover, at the very beginning of his presidency, Putin talked more positively about Russia's historic ties to Europe. Even as relations with the West soured in the 2010s, members of the elite were as likely to prefer a partnership with the European Union as with China. Tellingly, members of the elite prefer to vacation and own property in Europe, not in China or other Asian countries. According to surveys, elites also had gradually come around to the idea that Russia and Ukraine were destined to be separate countries, a view not shared by Putin.

In a personalist autocracy, the autocrat's personality drives key political decisions. Putin himself took the decision to start the war with Ukraine in 2014 when he annexed Crimea, as well as the decision to launch a full-scale invasion of the country in

2022. In both cases, he consulted only a small group of his most trusted and longtime associates. Putin's belief that, for historical, cultural, and geopolitical reasons, Ukraine belonged with Russia, his resentments against the West, and his sense of his own future legacy as a great Russian leader who gathered Russian lands all played a crucial role in driving the Russian war against Ukraine. Putin may also have believed that a democratic and pro-Western Ukraine represented a dangerous example that, if successful, could also provide an unwelcome and conspicuous model of an alternative path for Russia. War was the will of the tsar.

Despite the current confrontation, there is no fixed attitude about Russia's relations with the West in Russian politics. There has been plenty of variation over time, from person to person and leader to leader. The point, rather, is that the West often serves as a frame of reference for Russia—culturally, economically, and politically. With Russia waging war against its neighbor Ukraine, in large part because of Ukraine's desire to leave Russia's orbit and align itself with the West, Russia's relations with the rest of Europe and with the United States are necessarily hostile. This is not an eternal condition, however, and the pendulum will likely go back in the other direction in the future—although not while Putin rules in the Kremlin.

Russia's uncertain future

The walls of the Kremlin are more than 500 years old. Russia has been a great power for more than 300 years. Yet Russia's current political order, and its legal international borders, are little more than 30 years old. There is a striking contrast between the depth of Russian history and culture and the newness of its politics. Russian politics is therefore very much a work in progress. This sense of unpredictability, of multiple possibilities, is what makes contemporary Russian politics simultaneously so complicated and so interesting.

For many, this sense of open possibilities after the 1991 collapse of the Soviet Union was always a false promise. Rather, the Putin years have shown what Russia fundamentally is—an autocratic, imperial power that either represses or neglects its own citizens and inflicts violence on its neighbors. Russia's full-scale invasion of Ukraine, launching the largest European war since World War II, has cast a dark pall over the study of Russian politics.

The political scientist Kathryn Stoner captured the mood well a few months after the 2022 invasion with an article titled "How Putin's War in Ukraine Has Ruined Russia." Stoner noted that Russia had made notable economic and demographic advances since 1991, which meant that average Russians were living better and longer than ever, although an authoritarian government constrained further progress. The invasion, however, had wiped out many of those gains, as well as generating intensifying state repression at home and undermining Russia's standing abroad. Putin, she concluded, had "erased his country's prosperity in a feckless attempt to rebuild a doomed empire."

A fundamental lesson of Russian politics is that, more than three decades after the death of the Soviet Union, a stable and predictable political order has not emerged. Indeed, the hollowness of the very first article of the Russian Constitution— "Russia is a democratic federal law-bound State"—shows the failure to create stable political institutions. Instead, Russia has become a personalist autocracy in which even the political and economic elite are more courtiers to the tsar than independent political players. This will not change as long as Putin rules.

Given the importance of the ruler, and Putin's advancing age (he was born in 1952), there has been much speculation about who and what will come after Putin. According to the amended 2020 constitution, Putin can legally stay as president until 2036; he would be 83 at that point. Figuring out what comes after Putin depends a great deal on when and how he might lose power.

Personalist rulers who have served as long as Putin are most likely to die in office, which happens about half the time. About 20 percent of the time, they are overthrown in a popular uprising. Smaller percentages are overthrown by regime insiders or try to hand power to a successor. Looking at Russia historically, and setting aside the two leaders of a provisional government who only lasted a few months each during the 1917 revolution, most rulers over the past 200 years also have died of natural causes while in office. One was assassinated (Alexander II), two were forced to abdicate during a revolution or state collapse (Nicholas II, Mikhail Gorbachev), and one resigned voluntarily before the end of his term (Boris Yeltsin). Dmitriy Medvedev is the only one who completed a constitutionally limited term of office and then stepped down, but given his subordinate status to Putin while in office, this example is atypical in more ways than one.

If these patterns hold, Putin is likely to remain in power for quite a while longer, barring unforeseen health issues. Of course, a drastic Russian military defeat in the Russo-Ukraine War might change this, but even in such cases dictators are often able to hold on to power. As long as Putin rules Russia, the basic contours of Russian politics—authoritarianism, repression, economic stagnation, corruption, hostile relations with the West—are likely to remain the same.

On the other hand, Russian politics are famously unpredictable. This was brought home again in the summer of 2023 when Yevgeniy Prigozhin, another Putin associate from Saint Petersburg in the 1990s, spearheaded a mutiny of the Wagner Group, a quasi-private military company that Prigozhin had created in 2014 with Putin's blessing and discreet state support. The Wagner Group played a significant role in Russia's invasion of Ukraine, and Prigozhin frequently criticized the Russian military leadership and its conduct of the war. When it appeared that Wagner was going to lose its autonomy and be forced under formal military control, Prigozhin went into open rebellion, seizing a Russian military headquarters in southern Russia and sending Wagner troops toward Moscow. Although a deal was cut to end the rebellion before many lives were lost, the mutiny was the closest Russia had come to an armed struggle for power near the capital since the early 1990s. Two months later Prigozhin was killed in an explosion on his private plane, presumably at Putin's orders.

The Wagner mutiny was a stark reminder of the potential volatility of Russian elite politics. Most notable was that the forces most directly responsible for upholding domestic order—the security services and law enforcement organs—seemed paralyzed during the Prigozhin rebellion. As US Central Intelligence Agency (CIA) director William Burns stated, "What we saw was Russian security services, the Russian military, Russian decision-makers adrift, or they appeared to be adrift, for those 36 hours. The question was, 'Does the emperor have no clothes?' Or at least, 'Why is it taking so long for him to get dressed?'"

Thus, although Putin looks strong and unassailable now, no one knows for sure—including Putin himself—when and how he will cease to be Russia's ruler. This unpredictability is yet another example, and perhaps the most important one, of the weakness of Russia's formal political institutions. What comes after? We do not know. Russia's past suggests it will again be some form of authoritarianism. Political science research on what comes after a personalist dictatorship also suggests that is the most likely outcome. Some have suggested even more negative futures, such as the implosion of the Russian state itself, a scary prospect for one of the world's two biggest nuclear powers.

On the other hand, leadership change can often lead to surprising new directions. Frequently, new Russian leaders have introduced major domestic and foreign policy innovations. There is a good chance the next leader will have little if any direct memory of living in the Soviet Union and will have grown up at a time when Russia had a market economy and was much more open to the outside world, including information flows and the ability to travel. Countries similar to Russia have successfully left their authoritarian pasts behind; so could Russia.

Many have suggested that the twenty-first century will be the "Asian Century." Russia is the largest Asian country. Its relations with Asian powers such as China and India are likely to be of major importance. At the same time, Russia tends to identify more as part of Europe, the location of its capital and where most of its population lives. The often ambivalent relationship with Europe and the West more generally has been at the centerpiece of Russian identity for centuries. Perhaps the current period of estrangement will persist, but a return to seeing the West as the most desirable model for political development—what it means to be a "normal country"—is also possible. The West, for its part, may not be interested in reconciliation until Russia comes to terms with the war crimes it committed in Ukraine.

The most fundamental question for the future of Russian politics is whether society and the state can come to a healthier mutual relationship. The state has usually been both dominant over and indifferent to the well-being of its own citizens. Citizens, in turn, often accept this dominance but, to the extent possible, reflect this indifference back toward the state. The core paradox of Russian politics for generations has been that the state is powerful in relation to society but often ineffective at getting things done. The weakness of societal limits on the state's behavior leaves the state and its officials free to pursue their own interests. For Russian politics to truly change will require a different sort of elite—one that sees itself not as courtiers to the tsar but as servants of the people.

References

Preface

Harold D. Lasswell, *Politics: Who Gets What, When, How* (New York: Whittlesey House, 1936).

Chapter 1: Governing the world's largest country

The text of the Russian national anthem is at http://flag.kremlin.ru/anthem/.

Dostoevsky quoted in Dominic Lieven, *Empire: The Russian Empire and Its Rivals* (New Haven, CT: Yale University Press, 2002), 220.

Nicholas I quote in James Gibson, "Russian Imperial Expansion in Context and by Contrast," *Journal of Historical Geography* 28 (2002): 188.

On the Siberian Curse: Fiona Hill and Clifford Gaddy, *The Siberian Curse: How Communist Planners Left Russia Out in the Cold* (Washington, DC: Brookings Institution Press, 2003).

Bolshevik nationality quote in Ronald Grigor Suny, *The Revenge of the Past: Nationalism, Revolution, and the Collapse of the Soviet Union* (Stanford, CA: Stanford University Press, 1993), 88.

The Soviet Union as a chocolate bar from Stephen Kotkin, *Armageddon Averted: The Soviet Collapse, 1970–2000*, updated ed. (New York: Oxford University Press, 2008), 86.

On Putin's "historic mission": Vladimir Putin with Nataliya Gevorkyan, Andrey Kolesnikov, and Nataliya Timakova, *Ot pervogo litsa* (Moscow: Vagrius, 2000), 133.

On humanity "ending up in caves," see "Putin Says Zero-Carbon Energy Will 'Send Us Back to Caves,'" *Moscow Times*, November 20, 2019.

Chapter 2: Power, status, and greatness

Jeffrey Tayler, "Russia Is Finished," *Atlantic Monthly*, May 2001.

Putin state of the nation speech 2003: Vladimir Putin, "Poslaniye Federal'nomu Sobraniyu Rossiiskoy Federatsii," May 16, 2003, available at http://kremlin.ru/events/president/transcripts/21998.

Stalin on falling behind: "Stalin on the Ends and Means of Industrialization," in *A Documentary History of Communism in Russia*, ed. Robert V. Daniels (Hanover, NH: University Press of New England, 1993), 181.

Charles Krauthammer, "The Unipolar Moment," *Foreign Affairs* 70 (1990): 23–33, https://trumpwhitehouse.archives.gov/wp-content/uploads/2017/12/NSS-Final-12-18-2017-0905.pdf.

The National Security Strategy of the United States of America, December 2017, https://trumpwhitehouse.archives.gov/wp-content/uploads/2017/12/NSS-Final-12-18-2017-0905.pdf.

Andrei Kozyrev, "The Lagging Partnership," *Foreign Affairs* 73 (May/June 1994): 59.

Former Yeltsin press secretary quote: *PBS Frontline*, "Return of the Czar," May 2000.

Putin 2004 Beslan speech: Vladimir Putin, "Obrashcheniye Prezidenta Rossii Vladimira Putina," September 4, 2004, http://kremlin.ru/events/president/transcripts/22589.

Putin in 2005 on "geopolitical catastrophe": Vladimir Putin, "Poslaniye Federal'nomu Sobraniyu Rossiiskoy Federatsii," April 25, 2005, http://kremlin.ru/events/president/transcripts/22931.

Putin in 2014 on the Russian bear: Vladimir Putin, "Bol'shaya press-konferentsiya Vladimira Putina," December 18, 2014, http://kremlin.ru/events/president/news/47250.

Putin quote on "returning Crimea" from *Krym: Put' na rodinu*, documentary film, March 15, 2015, https://archive.org/details/youtube-t42-71RpRgI.

Putin quotes on Ukraine in Brian D. Taylor, "Has Putin Lost It?," *Riddle*, March 4, 2022.

Chapter 3: Playing economic catch-up

Stalin on industrialization: "Stalin on the Ends and Means of Industrialization," in *A Documentary History of Communism*, volume 1, ed. Robert Daniels (Lebanon, NH: University Press of New England, 1984), 181–182.

Karl Marx and Friedrich Engels, *The Communist Manifesto* (1848; London: Penguin Classics, 1967), 96.

First chair of Gosplan quoted in Vladimir Mau and Tatiana Drobyshevskaya, "Modernization and the Russian Economy: Three Hundred Years of Catching Up," Working Paper 0032, Gaidar Institute for Economic Policy, revised 2012.

Polish worker quoted in Timothy Garton Ash, *The Magic Lantern: The Revolution of '89 Witnessed in Warsaw, Budapest, Berlin, and Prague* (New York: Vintage, 2010), 16.

Yegor Gaidar on average growth in Yegor Gaidar, *Russia: A Long View* (Cambridge, MA: MIT Press, 2012), 22.

The Lech Walesa quote comes in many forms; one version is in "Lech Walesa on the Challenge of Poland's Transformation," *RFE/RL*, August 9, 1996.

The economist on "comically inefficient" industry is William Tompson, "The Political Economy of Contemporary Russia," in *Routledge Handbook of Russian Politics and Society*, ed. Graeme Gill and James Young (New York: Routledge, 2012), 251.

Putin's desire for "maximum oneness of state and business" described by Gleb Pavlovsky, interviewed by Tom Parfitt, in "Putin's World Outlook," *New Left Review* 88 (July-August 2014).

On Russian wealth abroad: Filip Novokmet, Thomas Piketty, and Gabriel Zucman, "From Soviets to Oligarchs: Inequality and Property in Russia 1905–2016," *Journal of Economic Inequality* 16, no. 2 (2018): 191.

On property rights and business in Russia: Maxim Trudolyubov, *The Tragedy of Property* (Hoboken, NJ: John Wiley & Sons, 2018), 168, 187, 14.

Former security officer, "holding everyone by the balls," quoted in Anna Arutunyan, *The Putin Mystique* (Northampton, MA: Olive Branch Press, 2015), 101.

Chapter 4: The failed experiment of democratic constitutionalism

Marina Agaltsova, "Russia's Unjust Justice," *The Russia File* (blog), Wilson Center, October 9, 2019, https://www.wilsoncenter.org/blog-post/russias-unjust-justice.

The Constitution of the Russian Federation is at http://www.constitution.ru/en/10003000-01.htm.

V-Dem's website: https://v-dem.net/.

Francis Fukuyama, "The End of History?," *The National Interest* 16 (Summer 1989): 4.

"Russian President's Address to Joint Session of Congress," *Washington Post*, June 18, 1992, https://www.washingtonpost. com/archive/politics/1992/06/18/russian-presidents-address-to-joint-session-of-congress/303246d0-5ecf-43b6-b39b-264e651c78b1/.

The 1977 Soviet Constitution is at https://www.departments.bucknell. edu/russian/const/1977toc.html.

Yeltsin resignation speech quotes in "Zayavleniye Borisa Yel'tsina," December 31, 1999, http://kremlin.ru/events/president/ transcripts/24080.

Yeltsin on Putin as a "strong, military man" in Boris Yeltsin, *Prezidentskiy marafon* (Moscow: ACT Publishing, 2000), 254.

Putin on "the benefits of democracy" in "Rossiya na rubezhe tysyacheletiy," *Nezavisimaza Gazeta*, December 30, 1999.

Putin on the fusion of power and capital in "Interv'yu ispolnyayushchego obyazannosti Prezidenta RF Vladimira Putina," *RTR "Zerkalo,"* March 19, 2000.

The phrase "weak strongmen" and the subsequent discussion in that paragraph comes from Timothy Frye, *Weak Strongman: The Limits of Power in Putin's Russia* (Princeton, NJ: Princeton University Press, 2022).

"Spin dictators" and "information autocracy" in Sergei Guriev and Daniel Treisman, *Spin Dictators: The Changing Face of Tyranny in the 21st Century* (Princeton, NJ: Princeton University Press, 2022).

On low- and high-intensity coercion, see Steven Levitsky and Lucan Way, *Competitive Authoritarianism: Hybrid Regimes after the Cold War* (Cambridge: Cambridge University Press, 2010), 56–61.

On the pathologies of personalist dictatorships, see Andrea Kendall-Taylor, Erica Frantz, and Joseph Wright, "The Global Rise of Personalized Politics: It's Not Just Dictators Anymore," *Washington Quarterly* 40, no. 1 (Spring 2017): 7–19.

Stanovaya on the legitimacy of elections in Robyn Dixon, "As Russian Voting Moves Online, Putin's Foes Say Another Path to Curb Kremlin Is Lost," *Washington Post*, October 14, 2021.

Chapter 5: Eternal state, changing society

Svetlana Alexievich, *Secondhand Time: The Last of the Soviets* (New York: Random House, 2016), 35–36.

Klyuchevskiy quoted in Stephen Kotkin, "Russia's Perpetual Geopolitics: Putin Returns to the Historical Pattern," *Foreign Affairs* 95 (May/June 2016): 4.

Rock musician on "everything was forever" in Alexei Yurchak, *Everything Was Forever, Until It Was No More: The Last Soviet Generation* (Princeton, NJ: Princeton University Press, 2013), 1.

Timothy J. Colton, *Transitional Citizens: Voters and What Influences Them in the New Russia* (Cambridge, MA: Harvard University Press, 2000).

Quotation "We were triumphant..." in Alexievich, *Secondhand Time*, 287.

On trust levels, see Vladimir Shlapentokh, "Trust in Public Institutions in Russia: The Lowest in the World," *Communist and Post-Communist Studies* 39 (June 2006): 153–174.

"The incoherent Russian state" in Stephen Kotkin, *Armageddon Averted: The Soviet Collapse 1970–2000*, updated ed. (New York: Oxford University Press, 2008), 146.

Putin quotes on the state are in Vladimir Putin, "Rossiya na rubezhe tysyacheletiy," *Nezavisimaya Gazeta*, December 30, 1999; *Ot pervogo litsa: Razgovory s Vladimirom Putinym* (Moscow: Vagrius, 2000), 167–168.

Polling data on Putin's trust and approval ratings and reasons for his support from the Russian independent pollster Levada Center, https://www.levada.ru.

Maria Lipman on the "non-intrusion pact" in Maria Lipman, "The Kremlin Turns Ideological: Where This New Direction Could Lead," in *Russia 2025: Scenarios for the Russian Future* (London: Palgrave Macmillan, 2013), 230.

Quotation "Our job is to go and vote..." in Alexievich, *Secondhand Time*, 80.

Shaun Walker on the Victory Day parade in Shaun Walker, *The Long Hangover: Putin's New Russia and the Ghosts of the Past* (Oxford: Oxford University Press, 2018), 33.

Joshua Yaffa on Pussy Riot in Joshua Yaffa, *Between Two Fires: Truth, Ambition, and Compromise in Putin's Russia* (New York: Tim Duggan Books, 2020), 148.

Putin on "perversions" and "Satanism" in "Signing of Treaties on Accession of Donetsk and Lugansk People's Republics and Zaporozhye and Kherson Regions to Russia," September 30, 2022, http://en.kremlin.ru/events/president/news/69465.

Senator Margarita Pavlova on women's higher education in "V Sovfede prizvali ogranichit' vyssheye obrazovaniye dlya zhenshchin," *Moscow Times* (Russian Service), November 13, 2023.

Samuel Greene on the dysfunctional state in Samuel A. Greene, "From Boom to Bust: Hardship, Mobilization & Russia's Social Contract," *Daedalus* 146 (Spring 2017): 125.

Andrei Kolesnikov on "indifference" in Andrei Kolesnikov, "Russia's Quiet Riot: Learning to Outlast Putin's Autocracy," *Foreign Affairs*, December 13, 2022, https://www.foreignaffairs.com/russian-federation/russias-quiet-riot.

Chapter 6: Tsars and courtiers

Stanovaya, "We don't have such an elite...," in Farida Kurbangaleyeva interview with Tatyana Stanovaya, *Republic*, April 27, 2023.

Henry E. Hale, *Patronal Politics* (Cambridge: Cambridge University Press, 2015).

"Security Council Meeting," February 21, 2022, http://en.kremlin.ru/events/president/transcripts/67825

"Soft legal constraints" in Kirill Rogov, "Pravila narusheniya pravil," *Yezhednevnyy Zhurnal*, July 22, 2010.

"They will attack you from all sides...," Sergey Kanev, "Posledniy spetsnazovets Sechina," *Medium*, May 14, 2018.

Boris Nemtsov and Leonid Martynyuk, *The Life of a Galley Slave* (Moscow: Self-published, 2012), available at https://www.putin-itogi.ru/rab-na-galerah/.

Fiona Hill and Clifford G. Gaddy, *Mr. Putin: Operative in the Kremlin* (Washington, DC: Brookings Institution Press, 2015).

"Hooligan" quote in Vladimir Putin, *First Person: An Astonishingly Frank Self-Portrait by Russia's President* (New York: Public Affairs, 2000), 18.

Putin September 2022 speech, "Signing of Treaties on Accession of Donetsk and Lugansk People's Republics and Zaporozhye and Kherson Regions to Russia," September 30, 2022, http://en.kremlin.ru/events/president/news/69465.

Kathryn Stoner, "How Putin's War in Ukraine Has Ruined Russia," *Journal of Democracy*, May 2022, https://www. journalofdemocracy.org/how-putins-war-in-ukraine-has-ruined-russia/.

Burns quoted in Greg Myre, "CIA Chief: The Uprising in Russia Shows 'Signs of Weakness' in Putin's Rule," *NPR*, July 21, 2023.

Further reading

Alexievich, Svetlana. *Secondhand Time: The Last of the Soviets*. New York: Random House, 2016.

Arutunyan, Anna. *The Putin Mystique: Inside Russia's Power Cult*. Northampton, MA: Olive Branch Press, 2015.

Belton, Catherine. *Putin's People: How the KGB Took Back Russia and Then Took on the West*. New York: Farrar, Straus and Giroux, 2020.

Connolly, Richard. *The Russian Economy: A Very Short Introduction*. Oxford: Oxford University Press, 2020.

Dawisha, Karen. *Putin's Kleptocracy: Who Owns Russia?* New York: Simon & Schuster, 2015.

Dollbaum, Jan Matti, Morvan Lallouet, and Ben Noble. *Navalny: Putin's Nemesis, Russia's Future?* London: Hurst, 2021.

Frye, Timothy. *Weak Strongman: The Limits of Power in Putin's Russia*. Princeton, NJ: Princeton University Press, 2022.

Gaddy, Clifford G., and Barry Ickes. *Bear Traps on Russia's Road to Modernization*. New York: Routledge, 2013.

Gaidar, Yegor. *Russia: A Long View*. Cambridge, MA: MIT Press, 2012.

Galeotti, Mark. *Putin's Wars: From Chechnya to Ukraine*. Oxford: Osprey Publishing, 2024.

Galeotti, Mark. *We Need to Talk about Putin: How the West Gets Him Wrong*. London: Ebury Press, 2019.

Garrels, Anne. *Putin Country: A Journey into the Real Russia*. New York: Farrar, Straus and Giroux, 2016.

Greene, Samuel A., and Graeme B. Robertson. *Putin v. the People: The Perilous Politics of a Divided Russia*. Updated ed. New Haven, CT: Yale University Press, 2022.

Guriev, Sergei, and Daniel Treisman. *Spin Dictators: The Changing Face of Tyranny in the 21st Century.* Princeton, NJ: Princeton University Press, 2022.

Gustafson, Thane. *Klimat: Russia in the Age of Climate Change.* Cambridge, MA: Harvard University Press, 2021.

Hale, Henry E. *Patronal Politics: Eurasian Regime Dynamics in Comparative Perspective.* New York: Cambridge University Press, 2014.

Hill, Fiona, and Clifford G. Gaddy. *Mr. Putin: Operative in the Kremlin.* Washington, DC: Brookings Institution Press, 2015.

Hill, Fiona, and Clifford G. Gaddy. *The Siberian Curse: How Communist Planners Left Russia Out in the Cold.* Washington, DC: Brookings Institution Press, 2003.

Hosking, Geoffrey. *Russian History: A Very Short Introduction.* New York: Oxford University Press, 2012.

Kivelson, Valerie A., and Ronald Grigor Suny. *Russia's Empires.* New York: Oxford University Press, 2017.

Kotkin, Stephen. *Armageddon Averted: The Soviet Collapse, 1970–2000.* Updated ed. New York: Oxford University Press, 2008.

Laruelle, Marlene. *Is Russia Fascist?: Unraveling Propaganda East and West.* Ithaca, NY: Cornell University Press, 2021.

Ledeneva, Alena V. *Can Russia Modernise?: Sistema, Power Networks and Informal Governance.* New York: Cambridge University Press, 2013.

Legvold, Robert, ed. *Russian Foreign Policy in the Twenty-First Century and the Shadow of the Past.* New York: Columbia University Press, 2007.

Lewis, David G. *Russia's New Authoritarianism: Putin and the Politics of Order.* Edinburgh: Edinburgh University Press, 2020.

Lieven, Dominic. *Empire: The Russian Empire and Its Rivals.* New Haven, CT: Yale University Press, 2002.

Lincoln, Bruce W. *The Conquest of a Continent: Siberia and the Russians.* Ithaca, NY: Cornell University Press, 2007.

Lovell, Stephen. *The Soviet Union: A Very Short Introduction.* New York: Oxford University Press, 2009.

Lynch, Allen. *How Russia Is Not Ruled: Reflections on Russian Political Development.* New York: Cambridge University Press, 2005.

McFaul, Michael. *From Cold War to Hot Peace: An American Ambassador in Putin's Russia.* Boston: Houghton Mifflin Harcourt, 2018.

McGlynn, Jade. *Memory Makers: The Politics of the Past in Putin's Russia*. London: Bloomsbury Academic, 2023.

McGlynn, Jade. *Russia's War*. Hoboken, NJ: Polity Press, 2023.

Ostrovsky, Arkady. *The Invention of Russia: From Gorbachev's Freedom to Putin's War*. New York: Viking, 2016.

Poe, Marshall. *The Russian Moment in World History*. Princeton, NJ: Princeton University Press, 2003.

Popova, Maria, and Oxana Shevel. *Russia and Ukraine: Entangled Histories, Diverging States*. Hoboken, NJ: Polity Press, 2024.

Putin, Vladimir. *First Person: An Astonishingly Frank Self-Portrait by Russia's President*. New York: Public Affairs, 2000.

Renz, Bettina. *Russia's Military Revival*. Medford, MA: Polity Press, 2018.

Robinson, Neil, ed. *The Political Economy of Russia*. Lanham, MD: Rowman & Littlefield, 2013.

Rosenfeld, Bryn. *The Autocratic Middle Class: How State Dependency Reduces the Demand for Democracy*. Princeton, NJ: Princeton University Press, 2020.

Sharafutdinova, Gulnaz. *The Red Mirror: Putin's Leadership and Russia's Insecure Identity*. New York: Oxford University Press, 2020.

Smyth, Regina. *Elections, Protest, and Authoritarian Regime Stability: Russia 2008–2020*. New York: Cambridge University Press, 2021.

Sperling, Valerie. *Sex, Politics, and Putin: Political Legitimacy in Russia*. New York: Oxford University Press, 2014.

Stent, Angela. *Putin's World: Russia against the West and with the Rest*. New York: Twelve, 2019.

Stoner, Kathryn. *Russia Resurrected: Its Power and Purpose in a New Global Order*. New York: Oxford University Press, 2020.

Taylor, Brian D. *The Code of Putinism*. New York: Oxford University Press, 2018.

Taylor, Brian D. *State Building in Putin's Russia: Policing and Coercion after Communism*. New York: Cambridge University Press, 2011.

Toal, Gerard. *Near Abroad: Putin, the West, and the Contest over Ukraine and the Caucasus*. New York: Oxford University Press, 2017.

Trudolyubov, Maxim. *The Tragedy of Property: Private Life, Ownership and the Russian State*. Medford, MA: Polity Press, 2018.

Walker, Shaun. *The Long Hangover: Putin's New Russia and the Ghosts of the Past*. New York: Oxford University Press, 2018.

Weber, Yuval. *The Russian Economy*. Newcastle upon Tyne, UK: Agenda, 2023.

Yaffa, Joshua. *Between Two Fires. Truth, Ambition, and Compromise in Putin's Russia*. New York: Tim Duggan Books, 2020.

Zygar, Mikhail. *War and Punishment: Putin, Zelensky, and the Path to Russia's Invasion of Ukraine*. New York: Scribner, 2023.

Zygar, Mikhail. *All the Kremlin's Men: Inside the Court of Vladimir Putin*. New York: Public Affairs, 2016.

Russian Politics

Index

Index

GEOPOLITICS
A Very Short Introduction
Klaus Dodds

In certain places such as Iraq or Lebanon, moving a few
feet either side of a territorial boundary can be a matter of life
or death, dramatically highlighting the connections between
place and politics. For a country's location and size as well as
its sovereignty and resources all affect how the people that live
there understand and interact with the wider world. Using
wide-ranging examples, from historical maps to James Bond
films and the rhetoric of political leaders like Churchill and
George W. Bush, this Very Short Introduction shows why,
for a full understanding of contemporary global politics, it is
not just smart - it is essential - to be geopolitical.

'Engrossing study of a complex topic.'

Mick Herron, Geographical.

www.oup.com/vsi

HUMAN RIGHTS
A Very Short Introduction
Andrew Clapham

An appeal to human rights in the face of injustice can be a heartfelt and morally justified demand for some, while for others it remains merely an empty slogan. Taking an international perspective and focusing on highly topical issues such as torture, arbitrary detention, privacy, health and discrimination, this *Very Short Introduction* will help readers to understand for themselves the controversies and complexities behind this vitally relevant issue. Looking at the philosophical justification for rights, the historical origins of human rights and how they are formed in law, Andrew Clapham explains what our human rights actually are, what they might be, and where the human rights movement is heading.

www.oup.com/vsi

INTERNATIONAL RELATIONS

A Very Short Introduction

Paul Wilkinson

Of undoubtable relevance today, in a post-9-11 world of growing political tension and unease, this *Very Short Introduction* covers the topics essential to an understanding of modern international relations. Paul Wilkinson explains the theories and the practice that underlies the subject, and investigates issues ranging from foreign policy, arms control, and terrorism, to the environment and world poverty. He examines the role of organizations such as the United Nations and the European Union, as well as the influence of ethnic and religious movements and terrorist groups which also play a role in shaping the way states and governments interact. This up-to-date book is required reading for those seeking a new perspective to help untangle and decipher international events.

www.oup.com/vsi